EVIDENCE F
AFTER DEATH

BY

DARREN PERKS

ISBN: 978-1659881325

First Edition, (updated April 2021)
© **2020 Darren A.C Perks**

Midnight Hour Publications,

Gold Coast, Queensland, Australia

TABLE OF CONTENTS

ABOUT THE AUTHOR

———— ❧ ————

D arren A.C Perks was born in Hammersmith, London, England in August 1968.

The Son of Arnold, a Stone Mason and Bricklayer, and his Mother, May, a Housewife.

At the age of three and a half, he emigrated with his family to Australia, arriving by plane in Brisbane, Queensland, in November 1971.

They arrived on the same Qantas Boeing 707 plane, The Winton, that was recently owned by John Travolta.

In 10 years of schooling, Darren attended 13 different schools in Brisbane, Sydney, Melbourne, Gold Coast and for a few months in Ross on Wye, Herefordshire, UK. near to where his Father, Arnold, was born.

Moving house was common for the Family because his Father would often have to travel to find ongoing building work and his Mother hated staying anywhere more than a year, as she grew up in a Military Family that moved often.

Darren has spent a lot of his working life as self-employed, and has worked as an Electronics Technician, Postal Worker, Music Store Owner, Taxi Driver, Paint Shop Manager, Antiques Dealer, Property Developer and Motor Dealer.

He is the youngest of 6 Children, is married to his wife, Marilou, and has two Daughters named Danielle and Summer.

Today Darren lives with his family on the Gold Coast in Queensland, Australia.

This is the First Book written by Darren and it has been almost 50 Years in the making.

FOREWORD

———— ⚜ ————

"I wasn't really sure if I fully believed in Ghosts, until one came knocking at my door…"

Although I consider myself a regular everyday person, who has lived a reasonably normal life, there have been many unusual occurrences that have happened to me and members of my family. In this book I will describe some of the many encounters that I myself have experienced or witnessed.

I grew up in a family where some members were quite spiritual or religious and believed in heaven and an afterlife, while others were not spiritual or religious at all.

My mum and eldest brother had always been open to the idea that the soul survived death of the physical body and that we were surrounded by the spirits of those who were otherwise deceased.

While my father and another brother, Jerry, would often say they didn't really believe in such things, mum and my eldest brother Rodney would go as far as to hold the occasional seance in our home and often attended church, as well as to later attend the Spiritualist Church.

I can remember as a young child, of maybe 5 or 6

years old, being sent to bed early so that Mum and Rod could hold a seance in the living room of our house, with friends. I could hear it all happening clearly down the passageway.

It usually started with clearing off the coffee table and giving it a light coat of baby oil. Then, all the alphabet letters and numbers would be placed in a circle around the centre of the table and an upturned glass would be placed in the centre. There was always a cross placed on the end of the table and a prayer would be said before those present would invite spirits to come forward.

Fingers would then be rested lightly on the base of the upturned glass and within a relatively short amount of time, the glass would start to move. I can remember all the excitement and squeals as the glass started to move haphazardly around the lubricated tabletop.

All kinds of questions would be asked as the glass made its way to letters in order to spell out words, many of which needed more questions to be asked before any sense could be made of the message. There were however some amazing results that came through.

Anything from playful and fun characters, who would accurately tell the colour of everyone's underwear they were wearing, to warnings of future events and even some information on missing persons, would all come through in a single session.

One particular night, a very strong repetitive message

kept coming through. The letters ABC kept coming up time and time again. At first, nobody really understood what ABC stood for until it was later revealed that ABC stood for A Bad Crash. The information that came through was that there was going to be a bad car accident and when quizzed, it was revealed that my Middle Brother Jerry was going to be involved.

It so happened that Jerry, who was only a teenager at the time, was about to head off on a long road trip the following day with his friend Teddy to North Queensland, which was some 2000 km to the north of our home in Brisbane.

Stunned at this revelation, Mum and Rod pleaded with Jerry not to go on this trip, but Jerry wouldn't hear of it and said he was going, right or wrong, and nobody could stop him.

Rod was so sure that our Middle Brother was going to be involved in this accident that he became frantic and did everything he could to stop Jerry from going.

Still, Jerry wouldn't listen and he left early the next morning.

A few days later the front door opened and there was Jerry, looking a bit defeated. "Well, we had our Crash" he declared.

Mum was so happy to see him walk through the door again and asked what had happened. Apparently, a day into the trip, Jerry and Teddy were driving along at about 4 a.m., somewhere North of Rockhampton, when they came to a fork in the road. They weren't sure which road to take, so they took a road and it turned out to be the wrong one. It was an unsealed gravel road and as their panel van was heading down it, Teddy, who was driving, lost control of the vehicle which flipped over and rolled at least 6 times.

Teddy was trapped under the dashboard and Jerry was thrown clear. Both survived, but the almost new vehicle was a write-off. Although no one was killed in the accident, it certainly was a bad crash.

This stimulated my awareness to the possibility that we could receive messages from the other side and it wasn't long before I started to have my own uncanny experiences.

CHAPTER 1
MY MOTHER, MAY

M y Mum was a very interesting lady. She was highly intelligent and very chatty, yet could also be very shy and lacking confidence at the same time. Her appearance was quite striking too. For as long as anyone could remember, Mum had always dyed her own hair. But the results were usually quite shocking as the colour always turned out to be bright orange or pink.

This was something I got picked on at school for as well.

I don't think I ever saw Mum's natural hair colour, but it obviously wasn't orange.

Mum also had a full womanly figure, beautiful blue-grey eyes and with her makeup and dangling jewellery on and in her earlier days, could stop men in their tracks as she walked down the street.

Dad always said, by 9 o'clock each morning, Mum was dressed ready to meet the Queen.

She was born in London in 1930 with a mixed English, Irish and Scottish background. As her father was a regimental Sergeant Major in the British Army, she had travelled and lived in five different houses, in three different countries by the age of 2.

During World War 2, her family was evacuated to Mauritius in the Indian Ocean.

It was there in June 1943, at the age of 13, that Mum lost her father in the war. He was heading from Port Louis, Mauritius to Nairobi in Kenya when his small boat, the SS Hoihow was torpedoed by the German submarine, U-181. The U-boat had received information on shipping coming and going from Port Louis from a radio transmitter in Capetown. The submarine sat out at sea, not far off the Mauritius Coast, waiting for Allied ships to leave the port. It was the second ship to leave that day, Grandad's ship, that was followed for several hours before being sunk by two torpedoes.

Mum knew her father was leaving that morning and was supposed to be going to school, but something told her to go down to the port and see her father one more time before he set sail. She could see her father briefing his men and then he turned towards her and waved goodbye. It was the last time Mum would see her father, for now.

Losing her father affected mum greatly. The whole family had to cope with the difficulty of being in a foreign land during wartime and it was now just a mother and her 6 kids to fend for themselves. When her mother, Ivy received the letter stating that her husband was missing, presumed dead, and how they appreciated his sacrifice, she tore up the letter saying: "That won't bring him back".

Of the 149 Persons on board, and many were young Nurses, including the Governor of Mauritius' Daughter, only 4 people survived and they were picked up by a passing ship that found them clinging to debris, days later in the Indian Ocean. The few survivors were taken to Montevideo, Uruguay where they were dropped off, after a few weeks aboard.

But Mum did get to see her Father again, for when she passed away in December 2006, mum claims to have been visited at her Hospital bedside by her father Edward Quinn, and also her father-in-law, Harold Perks.

Mum had only that day been admitted into the hospital because she was feeling a bit weak and was there for tests. She ended up staying in overnight and the next day when I went to visit her, she was telling me about her visit from Grandad, Harold Perks.

I asked her what she meant and told her that Grandad Perks had passed away in 1975. She said "Yes"... "and in 1943". I asked her which grandad she was talking about and she said "both".

I started talking to her about Grandad Perks, my paternal Grandfather, and she was quite adamant that he had been standing beside her bed having a lovely conversation with her, telling her how much he loved his grandchildren and even made comments about children who were yet to be born. These predictions would later turn out to prove correct.

I was unsure if Mum was under the influence of anything or just very weak and hallucinating, but the doctor told me that at that stage she was just a bit rundown, low on Iron and was only taking paracetamol.

Mum's health did deteriorate quite quickly over the next few days though, as she later on had a bad reaction to a blood transfusion and she had to be moved from the regional hospital to the city hospital where she would eventually pass away from complications of pneumonia 8 days later.

Although I never got to speak to Mum about the visit from her father Edward, she did tell some other family members about it and Mum said she was so delighted to see him again, just standing there at the end of her bed.

I should have realised it at the time, as I probably would today, but having visits from those who have departed is a pretty good sign that the ill patient is probably not going to make it.

Looking back at it now I should have seen the writing on the wall.

In the final 36 hours of Mum's life, she had an oxygen mask over her face and with all kinds of monitors and drips attached to her body. The Doctor said she had a bug in her lungs that was consuming her blood, leaving her anaemic. The Hospital tried every Antibiotic they thought may help, but she grew weaker by the day.

With Family gathered around her, I sat there holding her hand, which was hot to the touch.

She was wide awake and very aware of our presence though. The last thing she said to me while pulling the mask off her face temporarily and mustering enough strength to speak, she said: "We will all be together again one day".

And I totally believe that, since that day, I have had many visits from Mum and so has my family.

I will go into these visits in detail later in the book, as I have decided to write the book in more of a chronological order.

My Mum had always been a believer in Life After Death and she had read a few books on the subject.

She never really discussed it with me that much, probably as I was just a kid at the time she was getting interested in the subject.

However, I do remember quite well, at around 9 or 10 years of age, being taken to meet world-famous Psychic, Doris Stokes, who was visiting Australia from the UK to launch her new book at the time, "Voices in My Ear".

Doris said upon meeting us that she sensed Mum was quite Psychic herself and that I would later become so too. She also said that my brother, Rodney, was a Healer.

This was correct, as Rod was working as a Male Nurse at the same Hospital our Mother would eventually pass away in.

But Mum always did display signs that she was herself experiencing all kinds of paranormal activity and she often got premonitions.

I remember when I was about 7 years old, in 1975, when Mum started acting strange and would mope about the house and cry all the time.

She would literally lay down on the bed in the daytime and howl her eyes out.

Mum apologised to Dad, saying she had no idea what had come over her and was actually happy with everything, but could not stop crying.

It was something like depression and anxiety, but she wasn't actually depressed. This lasted for about 3 weeks. Then something strange happened. Mum was a smoker at that time and she was smoking a cigarette, whilst brushing her hair and getting ready in the bathroom.

She had just placed her lit cigarette on the edge of the porcelain washbasin when the cigarette suddenly spun around in a complete circle. Not believing what had just happened, she picked the cigarette up and placed it down on the flat surface once more. Again, the cigarette spun around like a propeller, but this time it was even faster and did 3 or 4 complete revolutions.

Mum knew someone was trying to send her a message.

The next day a telegram was delivered to the door, saying that my Grandfather, Harold Perks, had died of a Heart Attack, whilst chopping down a tree at his house in Weston Super Mare, England.

As strange as it may seem, Mum felt a bit relieved to get the news, as she now finally knew the cause of all her sadness and the strange experiences in the bathroom.

An unusual ability that my Mother had, was that she could feel someone touching her hair.

This was quite a common happening for Mum, and I must say I later developed this same ability, except in my case, I also feel someone tap me on the head, as well as touching my hair.

This seems to mostly happen when there is something about to happen, big or small, and often when I am sitting at home alone.

About the age of 12, my parents and I started attending a Spiritualist Church in Brisbane.

It wasn't all that unlike a regular Church, in the sense that we would sing hymns and say prayers while having someone give a sermon from the Bible, but it would also include such things as learning about Automatic Drawings, Automatic Writings, doing Healing and being invited to sit in a Circle, where people may experience all kinds of things, including Visions, Healings, and even an occasional Apparition.

Despite all this going on around me, I wasn't really sure if I truly believed in any of it.

I mean, I had met all kinds of lovely people and we enjoyed singing the hymns and eating the Cornflake Cookies that were made by the Pastor, but I just couldn't really see anything that fully convinced me of the supernatural.

But all this changed as I got older, when those around me started dropping like flies and the things that occurred soon after would affect me and my family forever.

CHAPTER 2

MY BROTHER-IN-LAW, PER

I n late 1981 my Sister, Vanda, married a Danish Man by the name of Per. (Pier)

Both Vanda and Per were on their second marriages and both had a Son about the same age.

In fact, they met because their two kids were in the same class at school together.

Per was very interested in the subject of Ghosts and Spirits and Mum had told him we had been attending the Spiritualist Church. He asked Mum if there was any way he could find out what his future job prospects were, as he had been working as a casual typesetter at the local newspaper and there was now a shortage of work.

Mum told him about something we had seen at Church just the week before, where you get two small squares of paper, write YES on each side of one piece and NO on each side of the other, and then hang them off the ceiling with cotton thread and sticky tape.

You could then ask questions and with a bit of luck, the paper with the right answer would turn.

Per became really excited at the thought and wanted to see if this would actually work, so they quickly made up a set and went about hanging the bits of paper off the ceiling.

To show how it works, Mum stood back a couple of paces and started asking a question or two, and without fail, she seemed to be getting a response each time with only the Yes or No turning on its own.

Per was quite excited about this and asked Mum to stand aside while he had a go.

As he asked question after question, there was no response at all from the previously active paper tags. I was there and they just kind of quavered gently back and forth with no definitive answer.

Mum gave me a concerned look as we took the apparatus down again from the ceiling.

She said to me after Per had walked off: "I don't like that. I don't like it at all ".

Not getting any answer when Per had a go bothered Mum deeply.

Australia was in a recession at the time and there was not a lot of work around, especially for my father, Arnold, who was a House Builder.

So within a few days, we had packed our bags and caught the Train some 1850 kms South to Melbourne, where job prospects were a bit better.

We had only been in Melbourne for less than 48 hours when we received a phone call from my brother, Jerry, informing us that Per had just died. We couldn't believe it and were deeply shocked.

Apparently, the kids were misbehaving and Per shouted at them to make them behave.

He then put his hands to his head and dropped dead on the floor.

He had burst an undetected aneurysm in his brain.

But that wasn't the last of Per it seems, because in the evening on the day of his funeral, Vanda was sitting up in bed holding their wedding photo when she felt a presence and a cold chill go through the entire bedroom.

She then felt a familiar feeling as a pair of lips came forth and kissed her on the cheek.

Vanda always claimed it was Per giving her a final goodbye kiss.

CHAPTER 3
MY BROTHER, ROD

M y eldest Brother, Rodney was born in England in 1953.

Rod is very similar to our Mum in the sense that he has always had an interest in the subject of Life After Death and this comes from the fact that Rod has himself experienced more than his fair share of ghostly encounters.

I met with Rod at his home in Brisbane today to have him freshly tell me some of his experiences and as usual, he was able to remind me of some quite hair raising tales of things he has experienced over the years. I have heard some of these stories in the past at the time when they first happened and some I only heard for the first time today.

As a child, I remember Rod being in the Australian Army based at Puckapunyal in Victoria. Before emigrating to Australia, Rod had been one of the Queen's Grenadier Guards in London and upon arriving in Australia he soon joined the Army.

"Pucka" as it is known to most Aussies is an Army Camp about an hour or so above Melbourne.

Rod would drive home often when on leave, the 1800 kms to Brisbane in his little 1970's Datsun 1600 car and in those days he did the trip straight without stopping, except for fuel and a bite to eat at a Road House Petrol Station or two along the way.

One particular trip, he had driven 1450 kms straight to Northern New South Wales and was just south of the town of Glen Innes. As he had a long day and a tiring trip, Rod decided to pull the car over off the road and get a bit of sleep in the car before continuing for the final four hours of the trip home.

Not long had Rod pulled over off the road, that he felt a strange movement as if the car was rolling or moving. He looked around quickly to see what was happening and saw that the car wasn't rolling forward, but was actually moving sideways to the left. He thought it very strange and quite impossible but it was as if someone had picked up the rear end of the car and moved it two or three feet to the left.

Right at that moment, a huge Truck came belting over the hill and came down upon Rod's car at great speed. Rod said that if his car had not have been moved out of the way like it was, he would have been collected by the massive truck and killed. He only just missed being hit by the truck by a matter of inches.

When Rod was working as a Male Nurse years later at the Princess Alexandra Hospital in Brisbane, he and a nurse he knew were putting their gowns on to go into Theatre.

The lady nurse asked Rod if he could tie her strings up at the back and he said: "Yes, just give me a moment to put mine on first". The nurse then came over and tied Rod's gown up, but when he went to tie up the female nurse's gown, it was already tied in a nice bow.

Rod and that Nurse were the only persons present in the room, and neither of them could tell who tied the strings that day. It was a complete mystery to them.

In the early 1990's, Rod was now working for Brisbane City Council as a Bus Driver. He was given a new Bus Route from the City out to the Pinnaroo Lawn Cemetery and Crematorium, located north of Brisbane, and then back to the City. The previous Driver had been a Chinese Australian who refused to do that Route any more.

One quiet day, Rod had driven the Bus out to the Cemetery and was just waiting for his time slot to drive back to the City.

A man in his 40's appeared at the bus door and when Rod opened it, the man asked if Rod was going to the City.

Rod said: "Yes" and the man then got on board.

On the entire trip back to the City, only one other passenger got on the Bus and he was also going to the same bus stop in the City.

As Rod pulled into the final stop at the City Terminus, he opened the front door to let the two men off. But only one man got off, the second customer. Rod went and searched the entire length of the bus, but the first passenger who got on at the Cemetery had totally disappeared. He had even bought a ticket.

When Rod made enquiries to the other bus driver about why he refused to do that Route anymore, the guy replied that while he had been parked at the Cemetery Bus Stop, he could hear hands banging on the outside of the bus. This had happened a few times and each time he got out to check, there was nobody there. This frightened the Driver and he said he simply refused to ever go out there again.

CHAPTER 4
THE GHOST BOY OF KURRAWA

I n 1982 I was now 14 years old and was a Year 9 student at Miami High School on the Gold Coast.

We lived in a 2 storey townhouse in Broadbeach, it was just Mum, Dad and I and we were in a great location as it was just a two-minute walk to one of Australia's best beaches.

I would often go there to swim in the surf on weekends with my Brother, Rodney, and I would occasionally walk to the beach on my own after coming home from school, just to walk along the pure white sand and listen to the rolling waves.

One afternoon, at about 5 pm, I had walked to the quiet northern end of Kurrawa Beach and decided to plonk myself down on the sand and just sit there, drawing pictures in a patch of sand that was very smooth and flat.

As I was drawing random patterns with my finger, a young boy about 7 years old came up and sat down beside me. I don't remember him walking up, but just him coming and sitting down cross-legged right in front of my left knee.

He was wearing only a pair of grey school shorts, but I noticed that they were a lot longer in the leg than the short-shorts we were all wearing at that time in the early 1980's. They were also made of a type of tweed speckled material, which may have been wool, and that was well and truly out of fashion and certainly not from any recent period to that time.

As soon as he arrived to join in what I was doing, I felt and saw the hairs on my arms stand on end, yet I felt a sort of feeling of love emanating from him. When I looked at his eyes, I was taken aback as they were very unusual in the fact that they had almost no colour to them, sort of like a very pale grey/ off white and there was something not quite right about him at all. He was ruggedly handsome in a way and smiled a lot, but I thought there was something about him that made me think he may have been mildly disabled or possibly even a deaf-mute because he never uttered a sound.

I was used to entertaining younger kids, so we took turns at drawing things in the sand for a minute or two. But after a short time, he looked up as if someone was calling him. I couldn't see or hear anyone. He then simply got up without as much as a word or a wave goodbye, took 2 or 3 steps to my side and totally disappeared. I was so shocked at what just happened. I turned immediately and there wasn't another soul within hundreds of metres of me either end of the beach and there was nowhere he could have gone. He just simply vanished as mysteriously as he arrived.

Only then did I conclude that I had played on the beach with a Ghost Child from another era.

It is my belief after all these years that this Boy had possibly drowned on the Beach, and probably circa 1920's to the 1960's.

Another strange thing to add to this story is that when I told a group of local people about what I experienced, someone later emailed me to tell a similar story that happened on almost the same stretch of beach. They told me about a group of school kids from the local Broadbeach State School in the late 1960's or early 1970's, who had gone on an excursion to the beach, located just across the road. Apparently, after they were finished on the beach and were about to return to school, the teacher told the students from the Grade 2 or 3 class to hold hands as they walked up the beach and headed towards the road they had to cross to get back to the School grounds.

As they reached the grassy parkland area and were leaving the sand, a little girl at the end of the line ran up and told the Teacher that the little Boy she was holding hands with had refused to leave the Beach and he had let go of her hand and walked back. When the teacher went to the back of the line, just a matter of metres behind, there was no Boy to be seen. A headcount proved that all Students were accounted for, but an extra Boy, that the Girl had never seen before, had been holding her hand all the way.

Chapter 5
Gran's House

T he first time I ever saw a person pass away in front of me, or any dead person at all for that matter, was the death of a lady we affectionately called Gran, as she was the paternal Grandmother of the girl I was dating at the time.

It was 1992 and Gran, who was in her 80's at the time, was a slim, intelligent, independent and proud woman, who lived just a couple of kilometres from my Girlfriend's Family in the southern suburbs of Melbourne.

We visited Gran a few times at her home and I took quite a liking to her.

Gran had lost her husband when their only child, a son, was quite young.

She raised her son on her own and never looked at another man again while living in the same house for about 50+ years.

But eventually, Gran's health started to deteriorate and it wasn't long until she was admitted to hospital, from where she would never return home again. When things got really bad, and it seemed quite apparent the end was in sight, her whole family including myself gathered around her bed one night and we all stayed there surrounding her until she took her last breath.

Her breathing until that point had been slowly getting further and further apart. First 10 seconds apart, then 20 seconds, then 30 seconds, until there was only the occasional breath about once a minute.

When Gran drew what was to be her last breath and the next one wasn't forthcoming, I noticed a complete change in her. To me, it seemed totally apparent, the split second of when she was alive and when she wasn't. It was more than just the stopping of her breathing, but that I could physically see that she had now vacated the body that was lying there and nobody was home.

It was totally as if she just got up and left before our eyes.

At the time I was living in a little town called Heathcote, in central Victoria, and it was a good hour and a half to commute by car back to Melbourne each time we went to see my Girlfriend's Family.

As her Father had now inherited the house, and it was just sitting there vacant, we were offered the chance to rent the house, in quite a good area, for very low rent, just so the house would be occupied. So in no time at all, we moved into Gran's House.

Just two days after moving in, I was standing in the

kitchen, which was in the centre of the old house, just facing the sink while peeling some vegetables for dinner.

I heard my Girlfriend come in from the front yard, walk through the front door, take heavy steps walking down the passageway and come and stand behind me. I then felt her hand touch me on the left shoulder.

As I turned to smile at her, I got the shock of my life, because there wasn't anybody there at all. It scared the heck out of me and I got an icy chill all over. Every sound, movement, feeling and motion of someone walking up behind me was perfect.

I then realised that it was still Gran's house.

For the short time I lived there, I always felt like I was being watched.

Things hadn't been going well for me there either.

I developed Pneumonia, possibly from the dampness and the fact that the walls were yellow from 50 years of smoking.

When I first came down with Pneumonia, the hospital at first thought I may have had Meningitis, as my neck became very stiff and I couldn't move my head.

A doctor made daily visits to the house for quite a few days and there was at least a two week period where we thought I wasn't going to make it. I was facing death at just 23.

It eventually took a month to get back on my feet, but I was very weak.

My business, a Record Store called "Penny Lane" suffered as I couldn't work and was losing money.

Then a nightmare struck. When we had moved down to Melbourne from Heathcote, we took all of our Animals with us. There was a big Rhode Island Red rooster, 2 geese, 8 pigeons, 4 bantams and several other chicken's. We loved our pets and set them up lovely pens and a roost, but they could all roam freely all day of the large fenced grassy block.

So we were heartbroken when we went out the back yard one morning to find every animal had been slaughtered. We never heard a thing.

My lovely big rooster had been hung on the washing line near our back door and his head and heart were missing.

There was a pentagram made of feathers placed on the ground, down near the back fence about 100 feet away.

The next-door neighbour said her Dog was barking at something in the early hours of the morning, but she told him to be quiet.

It was Melbourne Cup Day, which is held on the first Tuesday in November each year and we were having about 20 people over for a Barbecue at noon.

I spent the morning going around picking up the remains of all our pets and placing them in sacks.

It turned my stomach so much, that I went Vegetarian that day and I would never eat meat again for another seven years.

I was now beginning to become very unhappy in that house.

So I went for a nine-day trip on my own to Thailand to try and forget about it all and relax and recover from my Pneumonia.

But when I returned from the holiday, the whole feeling and mood of the house and my girlfriend had become quite dark.

I ended up having a relapse and now had a second, not quite as severe, bout of Pneumonia.

I felt I would die if I stayed in that house much longer.

Also, my now Fiance and I were growing apart after four good years together.

Even though we had even recently become engaged, I felt I had little choice but to end the relationship and move back to Brisbane, after spending some 10 Years in Melbourne.

CHAPTER 6

MY BEST MATE, PETER

I first met Peter in 1997. We were introduced to each other by a mutual friend and neighbour, Glen, because he said we had a lot in common and would probably enjoy each other's company. So Glen arranged the meeting.

I'm glad he did because Peter and I hit it off immediately and became best mates.

We had a lot in common, Peter and I, despite the 33 years age gap. We both had a Wife that was born in the Philippines and both of us had one young child each at that stage.

We shared a love of classic cars and buying and selling all sorts of goods from antiques to motorhomes while attending lots of garage sales and auctions together.

Peter was a big man of German descent, was also larger than life himself and he had a big heart to match.

He was about 185 Centimetres tall and weighed around 165 Kilograms or more for the latter part of his life, but still enjoyed a very active and quite exciting life, even in his early 70's.

His white hair and beard also gave him the look of a genuine Santa Claus, so kids adored him.

It wasn't unusual for Peter to find a motorcycle or a car for sale interstate and he would fly down and drive it back home, sometimes thousands of kilometres. He found a Honda Gold Wing road bike for sale in Melbourne one day and asked if I could help him book a plane ticket to go down and fetch it.

So I did and also dropped Peter off at the Airport. I later found out that the Airport Staff were reluctant to let him climb the steep metal staircase to board the plane, which was parked some distance away from the departure gate, so they boarded him last and by lifting him up in a Cherry Picker Scissor Lift. He was, of course, upgraded to Business Class for the embarrassment.

A week later he arrived back at my door, driving a VW Kombi Campervan, fully laden with car parts, power tools and a petrol generator, with a trailer being towed behind and the Honda Gold Wing strapped on the Trailer. To top it all off, there was a small boat turned upside down, resting above the motorcycle. He had been on a buying spree along the east coast and had travelled some 4000 kilometres that week in all. He was 74 Years Old.

I remember him telling me that not long before I met him, he loaded up his wife and baby in a motorbike and sidecar combination and then drove them from Sydney to Darwin in Australia's top end. A distance of some 3500 kilometres each way. They broke down at one stage while crossing some floodwaters that were over the road. The water was infested with Crocodiles.

I loved his stories of when he was a crop duster pilot in a bi-plane in the 1950s and how he would sleep under the wings of his biplane at night in the desert. Peter must have lived at least two lifetimes. He even had another child after we met, a lovely Daughter called Jasmine-Ann and I was honoured to become her Godfather.

So it was quite a shock to me and many others when Peter finally met his end.

It was 2004 and one day I received a phone call from Peter's Nephew, Steve.

Steve rang to tell me the awful news that Peter had just died in Hospital. I was stunned.

I couldn't quite get my head around it at first, as I had just been talking to Peter the night before and he was fine.

Peter told me that he had scratched his leg that morning against an exposed screw head at the bottom of his bed. It was an Allen key type of screw that had worked itself loose from the movement of getting in and out of bed each day.

He told me a Blue Nursing Sister would be coming over the next day to change the bandage on his leg. But the next morning he got a phone call to say that the Nurse was unable to attend that day, so Peter should go to the local Hospital to get the dressing changed.

So Peter went down there and had someone at the Hospital look at his scratched leg at the A&E department and they said it was weeping a bit. Staff were concerned because he was on the blood-thinning agent Warfarin.

They suggested he take a tablet to help dry up the wound, but within a few minutes of taking the medication, Peter went into a fit of heavy coughing and his lungs collapsed. He had an allergic reaction to it.

They placed him on a Hospital Bed in a corridor and set about trying to contact a Family member, so they could get someone to sign a consent form to admit and treat him. His wife was in Germany visiting her Sister and his Son was too young to sign. His brother, Steve's Father, had to drive up 650 Kilometres from Newcastle to speak to the Hospital as next of kin and be there for Peter. But it was too late. Peter had deteriorated quickly and he passed away later that same afternoon.

It was quite soon after this that I would start to experience even more strange happenings that would affect my life deeply from that time on. More amazing and disturbing than before.

I had many long conversations with Peter during our 7-year friendship and we talked openly on every subject. One conversation we had several times was about Life After Death. Quite frankly, Peter didn't really believe in such a thing and said what many say, "When You're Dead, You're Dead". I asked him why he felt that way and he said there was only one reason.

He said his mother was probably the most religious Woman you could ever have met. She went to the Catholic Church several times a week, went to confession weekly, lived as a good Catholic all her life and always gave what little money she had left to the Church. All this while being a Widow.

Peter said if there was any way a person could have come back to see her Family, she would have. But he never saw his Mum after she passed away.

I could see his point. It sort of made sense. But I then told him about the strange events that I had experienced and he knew I was being totally honest with him.

So we made a pact, right there and then. It was actually Peter's idea.

We both agreed that whoever went first, they would come back and let the other person know, somehow. We then shook hands on it.

Peter was obviously the first to go, and only a matter of months after making this commitment to each other.

I probably wasn't even expecting to get anything like a visit or sign from Peter when he passed away, I was still quite shocked and saddened by his passing and all I could think about was his wife and the young family he left behind.

But It wasn't long before I got all the confirmation I would need and then some.

One thing about Peter was that he was very punctual and he had no time for people who were late. He simply wouldn't deal with them and took it personally as if they had let him down.

If he said he would be around at my place at 9:30 am, he would actually turn up at 8:40 am and I would just be coming out of the shower and have only a towel on.

I could always tell it was Peter who was at the door because he would love to grab the big brass door knocker and tap it heavily 3 times with a long space between knocks, kind of like you would see on the Addams Family. I would often answer the door like Lurch and say "You Rang?".

I'd always have to make him 3 large mugs of coffee while I was getting dressed.

In the end, I bought him a special huge cup of his own, so I would only have to make him one big cup of coffee instead.

On the day of his funeral, I was running a bit late. The service was being held just over the Border, in Tweed Heads, New South Wales, but with the burial being on this side in Queensland.

The problem was that NSW was on daylight savings time, which means they were already one hour ahead of QLD. Although it was only a 35 minute trip to the service, it looked like I was going to be late for my best mate's Funeral.

The Funeral Service was scheduled for 10 am, which was 9 am my time.

Around 8 am I still wasn't dressed and was having a shave in the bathroom.

It was then that I heard the familiar three slow knocks, of the door knocker at the front door.

I thought that seemed funny and wondered who it could be. When I opened the door, there was nobody there.

So I returned to the bathroom, face covered in shaving cream and the same three knocks happened again. It was even louder this time than it was before. Thinking someone was playing a prank, I quickly bolted to the door and yet again, nothing.

This time I left the front door wide open and held open with a door stopper. I locked the front security screen grille door with a key and thought that would be the end of that.

After I washed and dried my face clean, I went into the kitchen to pour a quick drink of milk to get rid of the taste of toothpaste. The kitchen was located no more than 10 feet around the corner from the front door.

As I was sipping my drink, I was startled to hear the door knocker start striking again.

I was absolutely baffled and stunned. I then raced around the corner to see what was going on as the second strike hit. Then to my amazement I managed to see the knocker metal ring raise itself and drop with force to strike the door, right before my eyes. There was absolutely nobody there. Nobody was home besides me and there was no wind. Also, nobody could have reached the door knocker as the security door was locked. I knew then that this was a sign from Peter.

I can hear what he would say now, "You Mongrel, you're gonna be late for my Funeral".

Well, I made it to the service just in time and afterwards, Peter's generous sized coffin was lifted by 8 pallbearers and was loaded into the hearse. We all made our way in many cars to the cemetery about 20 kilometres North.

There, after a few final words from the Priest, the funeral home staff took charge and the coffin was prepared to be lowered into its final resting place. As the funeral staff gave a final lift and prepared the ropes to lower the body, one of the young staff members dropped his sunglasses off his head and into the open grave as the coffin was lowered. They rolled under the casket.

I saw the young guy give a sad look at his employer, who just shook his head in a disapproving manner.

It was obvious he wanted his new expensive Ray-Bans back, but it was too late. They are still there now. It is so typical of Peter, even in Death, he scored himself a free pair of new sunglasses for the trip. God Bless him.

Anyone would now think that was the end of Big Peter. But it wasn't, not by a long shot.

Only about a week or so later, I was laying in bed in the early hours of the morning, when I heard quite a commotion going on in the Kitchen. It woke me from a deep sleep.

It was an awful din of cups and crockery banging, cupboard doors slamming etc.

My Wife, Marilou, was not beside me this particular night, as she was sleeping with our Daughter, Danielle, in the adjoining room, who was poorly with the flu and had a fever.

It was around 3 am and I could only assume that Marilou was in the Kitchen doing something, like making a cup of tea.

That morning, around 6:30 am, Marilou came in and woke me with a cup in her hand.

She said: "Here you are, a nice cup of coffee". I sat up to take a few sips when she said: "What on Earth were you doing in the Kitchen at 3 am making all that noise?". I said, "Me? That was You, wasn't it?".

Marilou was adamant it was me out there and then said: "You even got out Peter's Big Cup and Your cup and put them by the Kettle!". "So I made your Coffee for You".

That was it. I now knew it wasn't her at all. Also,

Danielle was asleep beside my Wife all night and I was alone in our bed. Nobody else was in the house and all the doors were still locked. Nothing was missing or out of place. Just mine and Peter's cups put out ready on the kitchen benchtop. I was of mixed feelings about the incident.

I mean, I had asked for proof, the only thing was we were now getting Poltergeist activity in our home.

And I guess one must also consider the repeated Door Knocking on the day of the Funeral as Poltergeist Activity too.

I still believe to this day that each was a visit from Peter. But it wasn't over yet, either.

What happened a couple of months later still affects me when I think about it today, as it was very eerie and personal and I don't think it could ever be explained away as a natural phenomenon.

It was around the date of September 11 in 2004. I remember the date because I had been watching a 9/11 remembrance show on Television of the September 11, 2001 attacks.

I had gone to bed at about 11 pm and once again, this particular night Marilou was sleeping in Danielle's room as Danni was sick yet again. I remember being woken by something a few hours later, I couldn't tell you what it was, but I just laid there a minute or two trying to go back to sleep.

As I looked up at the ceiling of our dark bedroom, I could see something like a black spot on the ceiling above me. I would say it was located on the ceiling directly above my knees and was nowhere near the ceiling fan or flush-mounted ceiling light that was in our room. It also was not a shadow, it was much darker black than that.

In Australia, it is normal to keep an eye out for Spiders and other dangers, so I paid attention to see what it was.

At first, it was no bigger than the size of a large coin, but as I watched it, it started to grow.

About 20 seconds later it had grown to the size of a sandwich plate. A bit longer and it was the size of a dinner plate. I became concerned about what I was seeing and just laid there very still with the blanket up to my neck, just watching it.

It then changed in the fact that I could now look up through the ceiling and roof and see something like the starry sky. About this time, a very pale light with a bluish hue descended down slowly from the void in the ceiling, until it covered my body from head to toe. I thought to myself: That's it, You've Died!' It was quite terrifying actually. It was so not of this world.

I thought for a split second I was going to be part of an Alien abduction.

But I continued to observe and think while trying not to move.

Firstly, I looked at the base of the bedroom door to see if the hallway light had been turned on. It wasn't. I then glanced at the window to see if maybe there was a light from a car outside. It was totally dark. I then thought I had worked out was going on. I thought my Mobile Phone had lit up. But no, it was switched off and on charge in the bathroom. I was in a totally dark room that had a pale blue light coming from a black void in the ceiling. So I paid even closer attention to it. It is hard to explain, but while in the blue light, it was a slightly humid or moist feeling and there was a different smell, a kind of earthy smell about it.

The only way I can describe the smell is that in 1993 I had flown with a friend to Vanuatu. We arrived at about 10 pm and as we got off the plane, we both commented that it smelled like an earthy steamy tropical jungle.

This was very similar to the smell inside the blue light.

I was quite worried while all this was taking place. I didn't know if I was seeing "The Light" and it meant I was dying? Was I having a Heart Attack or something? I glanced over at the clock radio that was very dimly lit, and the time was now 3:14 am.

I suddenly remembered Peter and realised it must be from him. With that, I simply said in a very low voice, "If that is you Peter, I have received your message now. Thank You".

And with that, a few seconds later, the light disappeared and the Black Void closed up slowly. The room was now normal again. The whole incident lasted probably 2-3 minutes in total.

"Wow, was that a surreal experience" I thought to myself.

I had told Peter I had got the message, but I don't think I had got the right message at the time.

You see, I was thinking that this was more proof of the Afterlife from Peter.

But as it turned out, it took a bit longer to get the full message.

While Peter was alive, he had always wanted another child, especially a Daughter. Just 18 Months or so before he passed, his wife, Diana gave birth to a baby girl.

Peter was over the moon about it.

I told him that Marilou and I would like another baby, maybe a boy this time.

Peter said Girls were the best. He encouraged My Wife and me to try for another one and in August 2004, we started trying to conceive our second child.

We were not successful the first month but kept on trying. The following month, Marilou conceived.

Summer Madison Perks was born on May 31st of 2005.

We were expecting Summer to be born around the 9th of June, but she was born a little bit early.

The Doctor suggested that Marilou probably conceived about the 10th of September.

That was the night before the encounter I experienced. I think I finally got the message from Peter. He was telling me that a little girl was on the way and he would have been so excited for us. Who knows, maybe he had something to do with it? A little celestial help?

I am sad to say it in a way, that I never sensed anything from Peter ever again.

But I think he had done more than enough and certainly kept his end of the deal.

CHAPTER 7
MY MOTHER MAY, RETURNS

A s I mentioned before, my Mother passed away from
Pneumonia in 2006.

It was the 11th of December and she died after being
in Hospital for eight days.

The entire family was upset and shocked at losing
Mum. She was such a strong character that we had always
thought she would outlive Dad by a long time.

I had always thought that Mum would still be kicking
around at 90, at least, and that Dad would probably go in
his 70's.

My Father had worked very hard and mostly outside all
his life and from snow and ice to blazing sun. Dad also had
Angina, Colon Cancer, Type 2 Diabetes, Hypertension and
a family history of heart attacks.

I am pleased to say that Dad is still going quite well
now at 86 years of age.

I don't think the passing of Mum had quite hit me for
a week or two following her death.

It took a long time to sink in. My siblings and I got together to plan her funeral, picking out her final dress, and playing her favourite songs to find suitable music for her service.

We all agreed on Perry Como, "For the Good Times" as the main song and we chose a beautiful vibrant Blue Dress. We also had an open Casket, an idea we got used to in the Philippines, so that everyone could see Mum once more for a final goodbye. It was also Mum's long-held wish to be Cremated. Mum was claustrophobic, was terrified of getting in a lift and always said she could never be buried in a box, so we honoured her wishes. The Funeral Service was held on the 19th of December and Mum was cremated later that day.

It was on the 21st of December, just two days after the funeral and cremation that I was lying there, sort of half-awake in bed. It was around 6:30 am or so and Marilou had just woken up a couple of minutes before and was taking a shower to get ready for her job at the Hotel she works for.

Laying and facing Marilou's side of the bed, I felt the weight of someone come and sit down on her side of the bed. Nothing unusual, I was totally expecting it to be my Wife getting dressed, so I just laid there with eyes closed and tried to go back to sleep.

As I lay there, I clearly heard my Mother's Voice say: "I was confused before, but I feel a bit better now".

This shocked me into opening my eyes as quickly as I could, and there sitting beside me on the bed was Mum, wearing the same Blue Dress she was wearing at her Funeral.

She was only there a split second before disappearing, but the sound of her voice was totally her. I wasn't dreaming, she was there and she spoke to me.

It was hard not having Mum over on Christmas day to spend with us and play with her Grandkids. I didn't even feel like having Christmas at all. It was a very sombre affair that year. We had Dad come over on his own for Christmas Dinner, but we mainly just talked about Mum.

I think it was also the only year we didn't go out to see the fireworks on New Year's Eve.

January 2007 was now upon us and things started to change at a fast pace.

The semi-detached house we had bought as our first home had now more than tripled in price since we bought it in 2001.

I was constantly being pestered by Real Estate Agents on an almost daily basis, asking us to sell.

It was in late January that a Realtor knocked on my door and asked if we would consider selling.

I told him the same as I told all the others before him, that we would only consider selling if we got offered a much higher than the normal offer. I then told him a figure that I thought was very high at the time.

He said, "If I can get you exactly that price, would you sell?" Reluctantly, I said yes, thinking it wasn't going to happen, or not for a long time anyway.

Exactly five minutes later, he returns to my home with a young couple who had just arrived from New Zealand. He asked if they could have a quick look through the place and when I agreed he then told me they had already offered my asking price.

Another five minutes and I had signed the contract to sell, pending Marilou's agreement and signing when she came home from work.

So that day, I had sold our house without ever expecting to, it was a cash sale and we had 30 days to be out. I now had to find another house to buy in a hot property market.

We decided to use the opportunity to buy a bigger, freestanding house with an extra bedroom and extra bathroom, double garage and twice as much land.

It was going to be hard, as everybody was looking for something like that.

We got approval from the Bank to carry over and increase our Mortgage to fund the new place and spent a good two weeks looking at houses for sale. But most were either too expensive or just didn't feel right. Eventually, we found a nice home that ticked all the boxes. It was on a nice large level block of land in a quiet street, was only

5 years old and had a huge park and a lake out the back gate. The only two things we weren't sure about was the front door looked a bit ugly and it was built of a terracotta colour red brick, which wouldn't have been our first choice as most homes in the area had been concrete rendered, which looked more modern.

I told the selling agent we would think it over that night.

When we got home, at around 6 pm, a lady neighbour called Macy knocked on the door.

She asked Marilou if I was home and then asked: "Can I borrow your Husband for a few minutes as my Computer is playing up?". Marilou asked me to go with Marcy and look at her PC for her.

As I arrived at Macy's house, she invited me inside and shut the door. Her young son was there and he said Hello.

I started to look at her PC but was immediately interrupted and told that she had got me there under a false pretence. I wasn't really sure what she meant at first.

It was then that Macy told me something that would shock me to my core.

She said, "Your Mother has been talking in my ear for the last 24 hours!". "I just said that so you would come over".

I must have given her a weird look, as I was totally

dumbfounded. "What do you mean?" I asked.

Marce, as she likes to be called, asked me to sit down at the kitchen table and she made me a cup of tea.

It turned out that Marce was a Psychic Medium, one of great talent as I later found out, and she had been hearing my Mum's voice all day and night, trying to get through to me with a message.

I was told it may be best if I have a reading with her and was asked to choose a picture card from the deck. I am not sure if it was Tarot or something different.

She then proceeded to do a reading for me and started to write down the information she was being given. The Information came hard and fast and a lot of it was stunningly accurate and made sense right away. Some of the other information would be confirmed later that night or in the following days.

There were about 12 points made in all and I still have them on a piece of paper to this day.

The first one was quite amazing. Marce said that my Mum had just told her, that Mum had found a house for us and she had guided us to it. We were meant to buy the Red Brick House.

We had only seen one red brick house anywhere, we had seen it that day and it was the one we had liked best.

Marce then went on to say that Mum said the front door wasn't very welcoming and we should change it.

Our sentiments exactly. By the way, there was no way Marce or anybody else could have known any of this. We had only been home 10 minutes and had not told anybody about us even selling our place, let alone looking for a new house to buy and the realtors were with different agencies not near to our home. There were also no For Sale or Sold signs on our property.

In fact, Marce knew very little about us, period.

But some of the things that would be raised during the reading were simply mind-blowing.

The next thing raised was to tell my Dad, Arnold, to stop wearing that stupid hat!

This was very accurate, as after Mum passed away about 6 weeks before, Dad couldn't find a hat to wear when he went out in the sun. January is Summer in Australia and sunburn is a real problem.

Mum had a bright pink baseball cap with Maybelline Cosmetics written across the front and Dad had taken to wearing it every day. It looked terrible on him. So I knew exactly what Marce was saying.

I was then told that Ginger was waiting for Mum when she arrived on the other side.

Marce asked me who Ginger was. I said I had no idea. Apparently, Mum shouted at Marce and said: "He knows very well who Ginger is".

Marce then got told that I must call Dad when I get home and he will tell me who Ginger is.

I was also told that for Dad "It was not nearly his time" and that "He will do a lot of travelling before his time is due".

This part seemed quite unusual because my Dad was not a traveller at all.

I thought this was a big mistake in Mum or Marce saying this. I just didn't believe it.

I mean, Dad had only flown to Australia in 1971 when we emigrated, but other than that it was just Car or Train trips. Dad showed no interest whatsoever in travelling anywhere.

Well, it turned out that Dad developed a Travel Bug because from 2008-2015, my Father travelled three times to Bali, once to England and then moved to The Philippines for three and a half years. He didn't stop travelling until he was 82 years old.

When I did get home from Marce's place, over an hour later, I called Dad to ask who Ginger was. He said it was the Kitten that we had given Mum about 6 months before.

I said, "But Mum named him Chester".

We had given Mum and Dad a male kitten the year before and Mum said she was going to name him Chester. I then gave him the nickname Chester Drawers, because he loved to lay up high on top of the furniture. I hadn't seen that much of my Parents for a few months after that, as they lived on an Island, and I had no idea that Mum later changed his name to Ginger.

Dad confirmed this for me.

He said that Ginger had disappeared about a week before Mum went into the hospital and never came home again.

Well, we now know where Ginger was, because he was waiting for Mum on the other side.

A few years after Mum had passed away, Dad was sitting around just vegetating and not doing much. We felt he needed another overseas holiday, as he had really been enjoying himself doing that.

I convinced him to take a three-week vacation in the Philippines to stay with a friend of mine and also visit my in-laws. I booked him his plane ticket and sent him off on another adventure to stay with our Aussie mate, Jack in Cebu.

But two weeks after he arrived, Dad called me to say that he had met a lady friend through Jack and that he would not be coming back for some time. I was discussing with Dad about the new lady in his life and about where he would live and how to get his pension sent over to him.

Right at this time, which was exactly 6:30 pm, my

clock radio turned on automatically beside the bed. I had always set the alarm for 6:30 am in the morning, but somehow the AM/PM switch had been moved to PM.

As the radio turned on, it was set to a reasonably low volume level and was just slightly off an FM station. As I was deep in conversation with my father, I did not bother to get up and walk around the bed to turn it off.

As we discussed details about his new living arrangements and he gave me the name of his new lady friend, my Mother's voice boomed out of the clock radio as clear as day. She said: "Darren!" and it was not a very pleasant experience, as mum sounded quite annoyed.

I was so shocked that it sent a shiver right through me. I wasn't hearing things and it was so clear. To this day I have no doubt that Mum had used the radio to communicate her disapproval to us.

These kinds of occurrences, in my opinion, cannot just be written off as coincidence or lucky guesses or the like. By this stage of my life, there was little if any doubt that what was happening around me was solid evidence that we survive death and continue on the other side.

And a lot more uncanny proof from beyond would present itself to me shortly.

Danielle in happier times with her Grandmother, May.

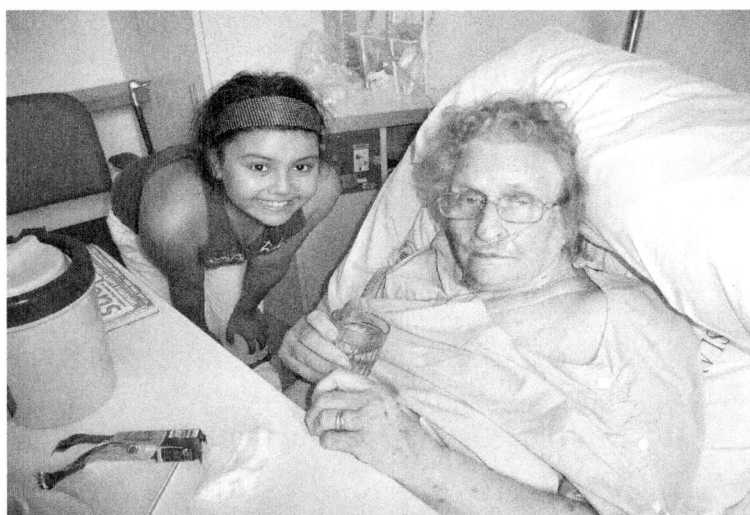

Danni with her Grandmother at the Hospital, just a few days before Mum passed away from Pneumonia.

CHAPTER 8
MY DAUGHTER, SUMMER

S ummer was born in May 2005 and is our Second and final Child. She was the most gorgeous looking Baby, Cute, Intelligent and very healthy.

A true gift from Heaven. Thanks to Peter.

Well, we visited my Wife's Family in the Philippines in September 2006 and Summer and my other Daughter, Danielle, got to meet their Grandmother for the first time.

Summer was 16 Months old and Danni was 8 Years old.

Their Grandmother, named Bebe, was in a Wheelchair when we arrived as she had a Leg amputated the year before due to Type 1 Diabetes. We were shocked to see how Mama had aged since I was last there in 1994.

When I first met my future Mother in Law, she was a healthy and well-built woman, young-looking and active in taking care of her kids and Grandkids.

So in 2006, it was heartbreaking to see her minus a leg, very thin and looking like she had aged 40 years.

But Bebe loved her Grandkids so much and would have Summer sit on her lap and get summer to dance for her as Bebe clapped her hands and sang.

She told us that she wished she had legs, so she could chase Summer around the house and play with all her Grandchildren.

Summer basically never mentioned her Nanna in the Philippines, I guess it was because she was so young when they met and not quite a Toddler yet at the time.

Although Summer did have a close relationship with Nanny May, and they did spend a bit more time together in Australia, Summer was only 18 months old when her other Grandmother, Nanny May, passed away.

Just before Summer turned 3 Years old, I was sitting in the lounge room at home with the TV on. I had left Summer to play with some toys on the floor of her bedroom, just about 10 feet down the hallway from where I was sitting.

I started to hear some giggling and then heard what I thought was her talking to herself.

The conversation went on for a minute or two and then Summer started giggling and screaming out loudly with excitement.

It was at that point that Summer came running down the hallway, ran past the back of the couch and started running around the lounge room, whilst turning her head over her shoulder to stop and look back at something or someone before running off again.

She was saying over and over "Stop it, stop tickling me".

I asked Summer what she was doing and she said that Nanny was chasing her. As we had talked about my Mother's passing openly in the house, I just guessed Summer was pretending to play with My Mum. So I said: "Do you mean Nanny May?". "No" she said, "Mummy's Mum, in Pilipins".

And then she said something that shocked me even more. Summer said: "She's got legs now and is chasing me".

I thought this was just her imagination, although Summer had never mentioned her other Nanny before. So this was something new.

I went back to watching my show again as Marilou came through the door from work.

It couldn't have been more than 30 minutes later that the home phone rang.

It was my Brother in Law, Marlon, on the phone from the Philippines.

I was surprised to hear his voice, as it was the first call we had ever received from him.

He said he had some very bad news. I knew it would be something serious for him to ring us, as international calls were not cheap or common, as the family was on a low income.

He rang to inform us that he was "sorry to say", but 30 minutes earlier, their Mother Bebe had died.

You could have knocked me over with a feather, I was very shocked at the news.

I was even more shocked when I realised that Summer had just been chased around the house by her Nanny Bebe, who had legs now.

Another time after that, Summer was about 4 years old when she saw my mother walk out of our bedroom, across the front entrance passageway and through the wall behind the kitchen.

She said: "I just saw Nanny. She walked through the wall".

Summer with her Grandmother, May, just one month before Mum passed away. Summer would soon also see her other Grandmother, Lola Bebe, who played with Summer by chasing her around our new house just a few months later.

CHAPTER 9

MY DAUGHTER, DANIELLE

D anielle, or Danni, as she likes to be called, was born in April 1997.

Being our first child, her arrival was the most amazing and exciting thing for Marilou and me.

We had both agreed to have Kids and we really wanted to have a family together.

Danni was born two weeks early as she was quite a good-sized Baby, but my Wife is not naturally a big person. I was present during the Cesarian birth and got the honour of cutting the umbilical cord to welcome our Daughter into the World.

She was also a gorgeous looking Kid and was a delight to raise, being sporty and active, had lots of friends and was always following me around like she was my shadow.

I realised that Danni was a sensitive person and also very intuitive.

It was apparent to me from a very young age, that Danni had also inherited the same sort of Psychic abilities, like the ones my Mum had.

That would soon become even more apparent as she got older.

It was a week or two after the passing of her maternal Grandmother Bebe in the Philippines in 2007 that Danni had her first real encounter.

She was 10 years old and was lying asleep in her bed one morning. When she woke up, she saw a little Asian Girl standing on the floor at the bottom of her bed. The Girl looked about 6 years old.

It wasn't unusual for us to have visitors over, especially Filipino friends and also many other nationalities that worked with my Wife in the Hotel.

Danni said to the little Girl "Who are You?". The Girl replied "Lola".

The little girl left and Danni went back to sleep for a while.

Later on that day, Danni asked us who was the girl that came in her room and stood by her bed?

We told Danni that there had been no-one else at home, no visitors and it was just us.

She then asked, "Then who is Lola?".

Marilou looked shocked, she went solemn and quiet for a while, then piped up and said: "Don't you know Danni, Lola is the Filipino word for Grandmother".

Danni said, "Well the little Asian or Filipina Girl beside my bed said she was Lola".

Marilou gave me a look, as if to say "It's happening again".

Danni has experienced some really amazing things Paranormal wise.

I believe she has inherited the gifts of her Nanny, her Mother Marilou and of Myself.

My wife has her own gifts and experiences, as you will read about later.

But Danni seems to be able to see things, some quite terrifying things.

She reminded me only a few days ago, of when a couple of years back when she was driving home at night and it was very dark.

Danni glanced in the rearview mirror and saw her Grandmother May sitting in the back seat of her car, looking back at her. She nearly crashed the car in shock.

Another time she saw my Mum standing behind her while she was looking in the bathroom mirror. These things could or should have really affected my Daughter, but she is like me in the sense that she has learned to just accept them, although they often play on your mind.

I don't see these experiences as bad. To me they are confirmation that Death is not necessarily the end, and our loved ones are still around us, possibly even guiding and protecting us.

They are visits from someone we thought was gone forever. Someone we loved and miss so dearly. And that is an amazing gift to receive.

But even having some sort of acceptance of these types of happenings, can only prepare you so much for things that are downright frightening.

Not long after the Lola incident, Danni was again lying in her bed late one night, but hadn't yet gone to sleep. She was just lying there with her eyes closed, face down with her head turned to the side. She felt her Mother pull back the sheet and doona cover and lay down beside her back for a while. It was only the next day when Danni mentioned about her Mum getting into bed with her, that Marilou said "I did not. I did not lay in your bed last night".

We automatically assumed that little Summer had gone and got into bed with Danni at some stage, but then remembered that due to the heat that night, Summer had slept in our bed with us, as our bedroom was air-conditioned. She had not left our room at any time during the night and our bedroom door was shut.

Summer was not quite 3 years old at the time. Danni said that the person who laid down beside her was a fully grown woman wearing an older person's perfume.

When Danni was 15 years of age, we allowed her to

have a sleepover at her friend, Montana's place. Montana only lived about 3 Kilometres away and was a nice Girl we had met in Danni's class at High School.

Danni stayed over Montana's House this particular Friday night and the following morning the girls were playing in the front yard when Montana said to Danni "Let's go up to the end of the Street, there's a Cemetery there".

So the Girls went up the hill to the end of the Street, for a walk around the Graves.

Not long after entering the Cemetery grounds, Danni saw a lady walk straight towards them.

The lady was senior and nicely dressed but was wearing old-style clothes.

As the lady walked close to the Girls, she said "Hello".

Danni responded back with a "Hello" as well.

It was at that point that Montana asked: "Who are you talking to?".

"That old lady there, that just walked past us" was Danni's reply.

Montana swore there was no lady or anybody else there.

When Danni went to point her out, there was nobody to be seen.

It was impossible for the woman to have walked off because the whole thing had only taken seconds and she could not have walked out of sight.

Both girls screamed and ran back to Montana's house.

Danni called me and asked me to pick her up early. When I picked Danni up, she told me about the scary incident at the Cemetery. I fully believed her and reassured her it was okay.

I was always interested to go there to that same Cemetery to see if I could pick up on anything.

But after seeing how scared Danni was, I was a bit hesitant to go there myself for a while.

When the timing was right, and it was a couple of years later, I finally did go there on my own.

What happened there that sunny afternoon will be a chapter on its own, later in the book.

Another uncanny incident took place in 2016. We had a beautiful white Himalayan Persian Cat named Ricky. He had the flat persian face with Peke Mouth and was beautifully ugly.

He was only about 6 months old when Danni found him in the driveway of our home, laying on his side and foaming at the mouth whilst convulsing.

Danni called me on the phone to come home as quickly as possible. I pulled up within 10 minutes and flew through the front door. But within 2 minutes, Ricky had passed away in my arms from a possible Snake bite.

It was a very sad time for us all as everybody loved Ricky. He had the most amazing and active personality, that possibly led to his demise and he would play with everything. We held a little ceremony for him and buried him under a nice garden in the backyard. Even our neighbour attended.

But that wasn't the end of Ricky, for within two or three days of his passing, Danni alerted me to the sound of Meow's coming from somewhere, possibly from the walls. I then heard it too. It sounded distant and muffled, yet at the same time I could swear it was close by. It was definitely the sound that Ricky used to make, very distinctive deep Meow's unique to the breed. This made us incredibly sad as it sounded like he was hungry and asking for food. We were heartbroken.

Later that night, I was lying on the bed watching something on TV. It was then that I felt the weight of a cat jump up on the bed, walk over towards me and lay down. I looked and reached out, but there was nothing there. It turned out that Danni also had the same thing happen in her room on the same night and she told me about it the next day.

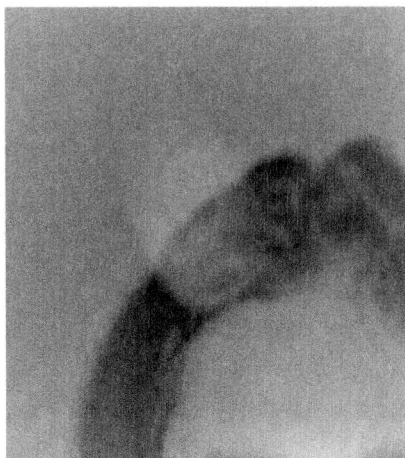

Danni with some of her friends. This was taken soon after Mum's Funeral, around Christmas time. There is a large Orb that appears just above Danni's head. Some see a face.

CHAPTER 10

MY FATHER, ARNOLD

M y Father Arnold Perks was born near Hereford, England in 1933. He is the middle child of 3 Boys and is a retired House Builder.

Dad served in the Royal Air Force and was a great Professional Runner in the 1950's.

He also dated famous British Actress Diana Dors, several years before he Married my Mother.

Dad grew up going to the Methodist Church in England and was not really interested in the subject of Life After Death or anything of a similar subject.

Although Dad was aware of Haunted Houses and strange Ghosts around the area he grew up in, he wasn't sure if any of it was true.

However, I still remember Dad coming home one afternoon in 1976, looking as if he had seen a ghost. He was building a lovely ranch style home for us and was mostly building it on his own.

This particular day, he was working getting ready to fit the guttering around the roof and was preparing to mount the wooden fascia board that the gutters would be mounted on.

Our new home was 56 feet long and was built about 3 feet above the ground at the rear of the house. Dad had a very long length of the heavy fascia board to lift into position, on his own, using only a ladder. He planned to mount one end of the board first, on the left-hand end of the house and then move down to the right-hand end to lift and mount the other end.

Whilst struggling to lift even the left end up and attach it to the brackets, and wondering how on earth he could lift the whole thing, he thought to himself:

"If only my Father, Harold was here to help me".

And with that, the right-hand end of the board lifted itself up on its own and hung itself beautifully on the edge of the roof bracket. Dad was totally amazed. So shocked was he at what had just happened, that he came home 30 minutes away to tell us.

My Grandfather, Harold had been a builder like my Father. He had also appeared to Mum just a few days before she passed away. Grandad was Cremated in 1975.

This is possibly the first strange encounter that Dad had experienced, but there would be more to come, for when after Mum passed away in 2006, Dad would get a few visits.

It started when Dad found himself now living alone in

the retirement house that he had just built for Him and Mum.

It was located on Russell Island, just a few Kilometres off the coast of Brisbane.

He had built them a lovely little 3 bedroom home with views of the bay, just 18 months before.

They could watch the Sunsets over the water, which is a rare opportunity on the East coast of Australia. Dad was 72 at the time he started building the house in early 2005.

The first thing that Dad noticed was that he could hear Mum calling his Name.

It was definitely Mum's voice he said, and he heard it several times.

As Dad was living alone now and I was busy building a similar new home on the Island, with Dad helping me, I suggested that Dad move into our house and sell his and Mum's place, as the single Pension Dad was now receiving was making it almost impossible to meet the monthly mortgage on their home.

So Dad moved into our house that was mostly completed by that stage.

It was the beginning of 2007.

As I mentioned earlier, we had sold our first Unit in January 2007 and had chosen to buy the red brick house, that I still believe Mum had led us to. Everything was going well until our Bank informed us after the purchase contract had become unconditional, that they would not have the paperwork ready for the new Mortgage in time for settlement on the house we were buying. They admitted they had been slack and the person handling our file at the bank had been away sick.

This meant that on settlement day, we would not have the funds ready to pay for the new home we were buying and we would be in breach of contract. I managed to get the Seller to delay settlement for another 4 days and he said he would not give another extension.

This was very worrying for us, as the place we had sold was a cash settlement, with a lot of that money going to the bank to settle that mortgage account. We could now be left with no place to go, have an unfinished vacation home without an approved new Mortgage and be sued for defaulting on the purchase of our new home.

I hadn't got around to telling Dad about our predicament that day, and when I turned up to work on the Island the following morning, he had something to tell me.

He said, "I had a visit from your Mum last night".

At first, I thought he had seen an apparition of Mum or something.

He continued "I was just lying in bed around midnight when your Mum spoke to me".

"It was definitely her voice, as clear as day".

He said she had given him a message to give to me and I would know what it was about.

She told him "Tell Darren not to worry, everything will work out alright".

This was very relieving to hear this, as I was deeply concerned over what was going to happen and this message from Mum was just what I needed to be able to relax a little.

I then had to explain to Dad what the message was about. He said Mum was looking out for me.

It turned out to be correct, as I knew it would. The bank manager was so embarrassed over what the bank had done to us that she took me out to lunch. Also, a new person was put onto our document preparation and a written letter of guarantee of a mortgage was issued to us.

It all happened just in time, but only about 24 hours before the house settled.

We have been very happy living in our new home and have been here almost 13 years now.

It feels like home and we see no reason to move again, despite sometimes having ghostly visits.

CHAPTER 11

MY SISTER, VANDA

Vanda was born in England in 1949 and was our Mum's second Child of six.

(Seven including our Brother, Adrian who was a full-term stillborn Baby in 1963)

Everyone loved Vanda, although she probably never really knew it. She was probably everyone's favourite Sister and close friends with all her siblings, but Vanda never really felt that happy with her life.

Despite being very attractive, and many said she was even better looking than Sophia Loren in her day, Vanda would always be unhappy with her look and often complained about her health.

But most would also agree that Vanda did not have a great life either.

It seems a lot of Vanda's problems came from the Men she was attracted to. If there was a room full of eligible Men, Vanda would always be drawn to the guy that had the most baggage and problems and he would often end up treating her wrong.

When our Family emigrated to Australia in 1971, Vanda chose to stay behind, because she had a newborn Son, Aidan and was in a difficult relationship. Her first husband was in jail and her current boyfriend was cheating on her. Not a good scenario.

Although Mum tried desperately to get her 3 Daughters to come to Australia, and we went back over there in 1977 and 1979 to bring Vanda to Australia, it wasn't until late 1979 that she finally decided to move here.

But her life was only marginally better here, as she soon found that her luck and the guys she met here were not that much better. As I mentioned before, Vanda Married Per in 1981 and he died of a brain haemorrhage in 1983. He was, unfortunately, a heavy drinker.

Vanda's health was also deteriorating, mentally and physically.

At one stage, around 2004, Vanda was taking up to 36 prescription tablets a day, after the Divorce from her third husband, who turned out to be a Swinger and Devil Worshipper.

We were so concerned for her and asked her Son Aidan to see her Doctor to try to get her medications sorted to a more reasonable level. It was around this same time that her Son Aidan also discovered that he had a three Kilogram tumour growing on his Kidney.

He had gone to his doctor because he thought he had a small cyst on his stomach.

It was promptly removed, but the cancer had spread.

Vanda lost her only Child just a few months after our mother had died.

Aidan passed away in early 2007. He was just 36 years old and left behind a young son.

A bit of happiness came to Vanda for a while, when she moved to Russell Island to be near Mum and Dad. She met a fun Dutch guy called George who used to play Keyboards in a small band that often performed nightly Gigs around the Island, so Vanda had a bit of a social life going to the Clubs he performed at. George also had a cool Motorcycle and Vanda would ride on the back, with her Maltese Terrier Dog sitting in between them.

Life was good for a while and Vanda seemed happy. Then one night, as soon as they got home from George performing at the Returned Services Club, George put his hand to his chest and collapsed on the floor. His Aorta Valve had burst and he died shortly after in Hospital.

We saw a decline in Vanda even more and she became withdrawn. We were later surprised to find out that she had Married another Guy called David and nobody was invited.

It was her fourth Marriage. David seemed a nice enough guy and he was very attentive and supportive of Vanda, but at the same time, he also had Asperger's and could not really show Vanda the affection she had always craved.

They Divorced within 3 Years and she then lived alone, although David would regularly come and check in on her and take her to Doctors appointments and buy groceries for her.

I didn't see my Sister much for a couple of Years, as each time we went around, we would cop a tongue lashing for how terrible her life was compared to ours. It was hard to enjoy going around there, but at the insistence of our eldest Sister Gail, who lives in Wales, I did go around and reconnect with Vanda.

After another good tongue lashing, she calmed down and we rekindled a good Brother/ Sister relationship.

And I am so glad I did, for on the next visit, Vanda revealed she was also terminal with stomach cancer, just like her son, Aidan.

It was in June 2018, and only about 9 months after we started to visit Vanda more often, that I got a phone call from David.

He had dropped Vanda off at the Hospital that Thursday for some respite care. She was only supposed to stay in for a few days, to give David a bit of a rest, as he was now her registered Carer. But on the Saturday Night, the Hospital called him to say that Vanda had just passed away. It was quite unexpected.

When he called us with the news, about 3 hours later, I was totally shocked once more, because we all thought we had more time with Vanda and we were going to visit her at her home on Monday.

Vanda used to like me discussing Life After Death with her. She said it gave her some reassurance and comfort of there being something to look forward to.

She really wanted to again see Aidan, Mum, George, Per and many other People she had lost during her lifetime.

She would also remind me of the time that Per kissed her on the face on that night, just a few hours after his Funeral.

I guess I had always wondered why nobody in the Family ever had a visit from Aidan after he passed.

I was kind of expecting something from him, but we never did notice anything.

Vanda wrote to a Psychic in a Women's Magazine a few months after Aidan's death.

Vanda gave no details and just asked the Psychic for anything she received.

The Psychic said she had heard from Vanda's Son, who had crossed over. She said his time on Earth was done and he was taken early as he was needed for something else.

That made sense to me and I didn't feel so bad about not getting anything from Aidan.

But the confirmation we received from Vanda when

she passed away was quite amazing and scary too.

When David called me to say the Hospital had rung him with the sad news about Vanda having died, he said he just laid down on his bed for a few minutes to let it soak in and was thinking about what had just happened.

He said he was crying and in shock.

About an hour and a half later after receiving the bad news, David said he heard a sort of tingling noise coming from his old landline telephone, located beside the bed.

He said it was the sort of noise one might hear when they were doing line work on the phone network years ago.

Just a sort of ringing intermittently, but with not enough strength to make it ring properly.

Half expecting it may be our Sister, Gail in Wales trying to call him, he picked up the receiver and said "Hello".

Next, he just couldn't believe his ears.

He heard a voice say "David, it's me Vanda, I'm not in any pain anymore".

He said he thought he might be going silly, but it was Vanda's Voice, he was sure of it.

David said she sounded so elated on the phone and he knew she was finally at peace.

Once again, David is the sort of person who wasn't sure if he believed in anything like that, but I'm sure he does now.

At the time of the call, Vanda had been deceased for well over an hour and a half and nobody was yet aware of her death, except him and the Hospital.

But Vanda wasn't done yet. She would soon show us exactly what she thought.

Vanda had left her will and estate in the hands of the Public Trustee.

We were already aware beforehand, of her wishes in her will, with the bulk of her estate being left to her Grandson, Justin.

She had however willed most of the family photographs and music CD's and Movie DVD's to her siblings to share amongst ourselves.

It was when we went to collect those things from her apartment that we had a couple of strange happenings.

I went there with my Brother Rodney and Daughter Danni to collect the things left to us.

Upon opening the door of her place, we all agreed that what a sad day it was and kind of surreal going into our Sisters place, knowing we would not be seeing her there again.

I set about boxing up the movies and music, while the

others gathered up framed photos and photograph albums that were placed in her TV cabinet.

After an hour or so of loading up the Car and double-checking every cupboard and drawer for extra scattered photos, we were feeling a bit peckish.

We had seen that Vanda had a lot of food left in the cupboards, and much of it would just be eventually thrown away. We made ourselves a cup of tea each and sat on the lounge talking about how sad it all was.

Danni said she was hungry and I told her I saw a packet of jaffa cake biscuits under the kitchen sink cupboard. So Danni went over and opened the cupboard door.

As she went to take the biscuits out of the cupboard, she let out a scream and grabbed hold of her neck.

Rod and I asked her what was wrong, thinking she had seen a spider or something.

But Danni said she felt someone's hand grab her around the back of her neck and they had dug their fingernails into her skin.

As she pulled down her shirt collar for us to look, we could see her neck was, in fact, red and with something that looked like nail marks. Danni was upset and wanted to leave at that point.

I told her to wait outside while Rod and I just grabbed the last few bags of stuff and we would soon leave.

Rod and I were looking at all the fridge magnets from all over the world and Rod chose one he liked for himself. As I started looking for one to keep, I heard Vanda's voice quite clearly say "Those are Justin's".

I told Rod what I heard and he said he had the feeling we were being watched the whole time we were there and felt Vanda was angry about people touching her stuff.

With that, we quickly locked the door behind us and left.

My Sister Vanda, being visited at her home in Brisbane by Danielle, Summer and Myself. Vanda had just started to lose weight due to Stomach Cancer. She survived for another 18 Months.

This was the last picture taken of our beloved Sister, Vanda, who called her Ex. Husband and Carer, David, on the Phone (Landline) several hours after she died from stomach cancer.

She told David: *"David, it's Me, Vanda !", " I'm not in any Pain anymore"*.

CHAPTER 12
MY SISTER, JEN

Jennifer was born in England in 1951 and was Mum's third child. She is the youngest of my Sisters.

Jen has also had some strange encounters, as she was only telling me today. A few years back now, Jen was looking after her daughter, Kathryn's house in the Brisbane suburb of Camp Hill.

As Kathryn was spending time living in her other home in South Africa with her Husband and Kids, Jen moved into the restored old home as a sort of live-in caretaker. The property was quite old and on its corner position in the long-established area, it had once been an old Police Station with holding cells and/or a Jail.

Whilst living there, Jen encountered several unusual occurrences that can only be described as bizarre. One time, She saw a man dressed in a tuxedo style Jacket, smoking a large cigar and holding a glass of Whiskey or Brandy.

He walked straight past Jen holding the glass in his hand and headed out to what would have been the old Verandah area of the building. Jen said there was an overwhelming smell of Liquor and Cigar Tobacco throughout the house when he appeared. The man looked to be wearing period clothes from about the 1920s to possibly 1940s and it is unclear whether or not he actually saw Jen there, but did not make eye contact and just kept walking outside.

It would have been like seeing perfectly into the past and Jen feels there is some sort of residual energy left behind in the building. Another thing to add is that before Kathryn and her husband purchased the property, another interested party, a woman, had to visit the place twice as she was not really sure what to think as the house gave her a funny feeling that there was some sort of bad energy there. On her second visit, and still seriously considering buying the old house, the lady decided not to buy it based on the bad vibes she got from the property. She believed there was something not nice still living in the house.

However, Jen said it was lovely living there and it was a beautiful home, with the exception of one other thing-The strange smell of Cabbage being cooked on a stove that frequently arose around the house. We all know that Cabbage boiling away can give off a distinct smell and Jen could clearly smell this on several occasions, despite her and the next-door neighbours not cooking anything like that at the time.

Something else that Jen was discussing with me today is the weird and unexplainable happening that took place when she and some friends went on a tour of Boggo Road

Gaol on Brisbane's Southside.

The Jail at Boggo Road was a notorious place of punishment, riots and death in its long history since Victorian times. Opened around 1880, it served Queensland for over 100 years and was the place where 42 Hangings took place up until 1913.

When Jen and her friends booked the tour, they were unaware that it was going to be a tour of Murderer's cells and other morbid and macabre displays. But it was when they took pictures of themselves at those locations that things turned out wrong.

Jen had posed for photographs with the group of people she went with, in several of the shots.

Pictures were taken by friends with both a mobile phone and a handheld digital camera.

But when the pictures were viewed later, Jen did not appear in any of the pictures.

She was not blurry or standing outside the group, but not there at all, or even you could say, invisible.

I have heard of an incident like this before, where a photo was taken of a person standing in front of an old wishing well in Central Victoria. In the picture, you can only see one shoe at the bottom, because a large spirit figure got in front of the person posing while the film camera was taking the shot, and amazingly the person posing could not be seen, just a slight mist where they were standing and their shoe only, visible at the bottom.

The incredible thing about this is that when this happens, the living subject posing for the picture can become invisible or completely transparent as if nobody was standing there at all.

CHAPTER 13

MY WIFE, MARILOU

I met Marielita through her Aunt, Teresa who lived near my family on the Gold Coast.

It was 1993 when Mum introduced me to Teresa and her Husband, Alick as they had met at an auction house that I visited weekly. Alick was a retired Car Dealer and he would later teach me a fair bit about the business.

Teresa was his Wife of many years and said she was originally from the Philippines.

I had always wanted to visit the Philippines as I previously worked with quite a few Filipina's at Australia Post and had always found them to be a bubbly and jolly lot of people. As I had visited Thailand and Vanuatu that previous year, I found I still had the travel bug and was planning to go to the Philippines as my next adventure.

When I told Teresa that I was thinking of visiting her Country, she suggested that I could write to one of her nieces, so that I would have someone I knew over there. She also suggested that I visit her home city of Cebu, as well as just visiting Manila.

She gave me the Family's address and I wrote a letter to them. A few weeks later I received a reply from the younger of the two girls, Marielita.

We corresponded for months and got along really well, exchanging many letters.

When I actually visited the family in June 1994, "Marilou" was so shocked to see how tall I was in person, that she ran a mile. Her Parents had to greet me ät the airport instead and Marilou had to be found and brought back to the Jeepney to meet me.

She soon settled down and we started to spend time together, although we always had many "Chaperone's" always keeping an eye on us. That didn't deter me though and we really were getting along well by the end of my two week's stay in Cebu and I knew I was falling in love. So I asked Marilou to come and visit me Down Under.

Upon my return to Australia, it took 18 months to get Marilou a visa to visit Australia, but it was a Fiance Visa, which meant if we got married during her 6 month stay, that Marilou could remain in Australia permanently.

So she eventually arrived in January 1996 and we were married in June.

Marilou started off by staying at her Aunt Teresa's house upon arrival, while we started dating.

Life was unusual for Marilou in Australia, as she found everything different, from the food, to the transport, to our culture and this was all quite a big shock for her. It was nothing like the home she was used to.

When I picked Marilou up at Brisbane Airport, she almost refused to get in the car.

I drove a Ford Falcon Station Wagon/ Estate Car at the time.

Marilou thought it was a Funeral Car, as nobody owns a Station Wagon in the Philippines.

But things settled down reasonably well and quickly as Marilou started to embrace Aussie Culture, even as far as following the Football and eating Meat Pies.

When Danielle was born in April 1997, we were a lovely young family and life was good.

I had called Papa, Marilou's Father in Cebu to advise him of Danielle's Birth.

He at first thought we had a Boy as he said: "Danielle is a Boy's name".

I said: "No, that's Daniel". He was so pleased and excited to hear about having a new Granddaughter and he wished us all well.

Danielle was still only a Baby, when we received the call from my Brother in Law, Marlon, to say that Papa had died.

Papa Lope had just come home from a long day's work as a Jeepney Driver.

He just sat on the couch and passed away. It was very unexpected.

It was on the day of Papa's Funeral that Marilou came to me and asked me to see if I could notice anything strange. I was taken to a part of our Townhouse we lived in at the time.

There, in a certain section of the house was a cold spot. The air was icy cold in an area about the size of an old phone box. But even more strange was the intense fragrance of freshly cut flowers that filled the air.

It had the chill and perfume of walking into a florist shop.

Marilou told me this was a custom of Filipino's that they believed in, that when a dead person came to visit you, there would be a strong smell of flowers in the house.

Well I experienced it alright and I believe in that custom now too.

I also noticed that my wife had some of the paranormal sensing ability that I had.

When Marce had given me a reading that time at her house, when my mum came through, she told me: "Your wife is quite Psychic too, but doesn't like to acknowledge it".

I would start to notice this myself as the years went by.

After My Mother died in late 2006, things of a paranormal nature seemed to reach new heights. Although I had experienced incredible things that I put down to Peter's passing in 2004, it was Mum's death that seemed to bring a climax to the encounters.

While sleeping beside me in bed one night in 2007, and we had not long moved into our new home, Marilou woke me up about 1 am to say that she had just seen my Mum in a very vivid dream. She turned the light on and sat there describing it to me in great detail and it caught my attention.

Marilou said she had seen Mum sitting on a park bench with another older man, and it was set in the most beautiful garden you could ever imagine. She said the beauty was indescribable.

Anyway, she said that Mum had been sitting and waiting on this old bench for Marilou to come along. Mum spoke to her momentarily and gave Marilou a beautiful big smile. She said Mum looked absolutely radiant.

When Marilou described the older Gentleman sitting next to her, she described to a tee Mum's older Brother Eric who had passed not all that long before Mum.

Eric had lived in England, and Marilou had never seen a picture of him before.

When I eventually showed Marilou a picture of Uncle Eric, she said it looked very much like the man she saw sitting on the bench beside Mum.

I would normally not give all that much attention to just a dream, but there were two other strange things about it. Firstly, Marilou can still remember every detail about it and said she wasn't sure if she was actually asleep at the time, or awake but in a dreamlike state. She said it was so realistic.

The second thing that still has me wondering, is that the following morning we were all having breakfast together at the dining table.

Danielle said that she'd had a really amazing dream last night.

I asked her what it was about. She started off saying: "I saw Nanny sitting on a park bench with another man...." I almost dropped my coffee.

I asked her where this bench was located and she said: "In this amazing Garden...."

Both my wife and daughter had the same dream on the same night.

Danni's Bedroom is down the other end of the house and she could not have known about the conversation Marilou and I had about her dream at 1 am.

So I let the girls compare notes and yes, they had both had the same dream. Or visit.

CHAPTER 14
PENNYWEIGHT FLAT CEMETERY

⸎

The Pennyweight Flat Children's Cemetery is located just an hour and a half, or 105 km north of Melbourne, Victoria and is situated at Moonlight Flat, between the towns of Chewton and Castlemaine.

It is a sad reminder of the harshness of the gold mining days of the 1850's in central Victoria, as the graves of over 200 goldfields children are buried in this peaceful yet heartbreaking spot.

We have owned property nearby for over 20 years and we always make it a point to visit the cemetery each time we visit the area.

Pennyweight Flat was so named as there was only a Pennies weight worth of gold found there and the miners knew that if this site was used for burials, it was likely to remain undisturbed.

Between late 1851 and 1857, it is thought that over 200, up to 220 children, were buried on this site which was exclusively for children.

The conditions were harsh in those days, with

children of the gold miners dying from influenza, dysentery, snakebite and drowning in water filled mining holes, which were among just some of the causes.

I guess all cemeteries are sad places, but a place that is exclusively for the graves of children takes the grief from loss to a whole other level, as losing a child must be the hardest thing for any parent to cope with.

Having been an antique's dealer and with a strong interest in history from the past, I really love visiting historic sites and soaking up the atmosphere. The grounds around these towns are full of old bottles and broken English china from early Victorian times and the old buildings from the gold mining days still stand strong as testament to when Australia was young, a place for adventurous pioneers and tough people who endured terrible hardship just to get here, let alone survive and make at least a living, if not a fortune.

In 2017, on our last road trip some 1850 km down to Victoria, we made a point of once again visiting the Children's Cemetery.

It had stuck with me and my family since our last visit and we vowed to go there again on this trip.

When we arrived, it was a cool but sunny day and with nice fluffy white clouds. We parked our Jeep across the road from the entrance gate and made a slow sombre walk up the slight incline towards the trees in the centre and to the first few scattered graves, many of which are not marked, while others have just their outline made in rocks.

We took a respectful slow and quiet walk around the flat in an anti-clockwise direction.

There were the usual famous graves from rich families that still had readable names and dates, and many more paupers children's graves that may have once upon a time had a wooden cross or homemade headstone that has not survived the ravages of time.

The names were English, Irish, Scottish and some had Chinese characters.

People from all over the world had made their way to this land to try to make their fortune, including many Chinese. Some struck it rich, others returned penniless, some just became drunkards, while others never returned at all.

Something that has never been lost on me is the amount of sorrow that was shown and the amount of tears that would have been shed at this site, by the many that saw their dreams end in heartbreak. It's hard not to feel for their loss, even 170 years later.

Anyway, we must have spent at least 30 minutes or more walking around to every visible grave. Marilou and the girls were a bit behind me taking some pictures as I strolled on ahead.

I was thinking how peaceful it all was and how the

people from those days would be stunned at today's advancements. It was at this point, as I was starting to get closer to the exit gate, that I could have sworn I felt something touch the fingers on my right hand.

I dismissed it as a fly, or some other insect touching me, but as I walked slowly forwards, yet again I felt a very light touch of my palm and fingertips. It wasn't smooth but a little rough like dry dirty fingers. I looked at my hand but couldn't see anything.

But several times, I felt something or multiple things touch my hand. I thought I wouldn't say anything to the girls, in case I spooked them.

Danni caught up to me when I was only about 20 metres from the gate and she said: "Can we go now?". I said "Yes" and we all made our way back to the Jeep.

When we had all returned to the car and closed the doors, Danni let out a big sigh of relief.

I asked her what was the matter and she said: "That was freaky!"

"What was freaky?" I asked her.

She said that while she was walking around, she felt little fingers touching her hands and not only that but could hear kids giggling.

I told Danni I had felt the fingers touching my hand too, but wasn't really sure what that sensation was at first until she confirmed it.

We still love that place and talk about it often. But we feel a bit differently about it now.

CHAPTER 15

THE GHOST CAR

I n the early 2000's, I bought my first PC from a garage sale and started selling things on eBay.

These were great times as you could put almost anything for sale on the Internet and get ridiculously good money for it.

I had just started to dabble with selling some of my cars online, which was going quite well and I was approached to list some vehicles for my mate Kevin, who was a Tow Truck operator.

I had known Kev for about 7 years at the time and his job was picking up unwanted Cars for scrap metal. Customers would call to say they had an old car or wreck sitting around that they no longer and Kevin would pick it up and take to the Scrapyard.

But one person's junk is another's jewels, and he was picking up some complete and running vehicles that were a bit too good to crush.

So we decided to keep aside some rarer or collectable cars to put up for auction online, instead of squashing them.

This worked well for a time but towards the end, we got too many people bidding and winning the auction, who had no intention of paying for them.

In 2004, Kev brought an interesting and rare car to the holding yard. It was a Merkur XR-2 turbo, a German sports car based on the Ford Sierra Cosworth. Apparently, the car had been abandoned under a Hi-rise building, where it had sat covered in dust for well over 2 years.

The building management had given the car away, to be removed as it was abandoned.

The owner, who was visiting from overseas had bought the car and then had disappeared.

When I first saw the car, I knew of its rarity and thought it an ideal proposition to be auctioned.

When I went down to the holding yard to take pictures of it, I looked the car over and I had sat inside it, checking the mileage and overall condition for the online advert.

There was nobody else around and I proceeded to take a dozen or more pictures of the car from every angle. I was using an early 4-megapixel digital camera.

Later back at home, I uploaded the pictures to my PC and started to look through the pictures to find the best "Money Shots".

But with the very first pictures, I was taken aback, as there appeared to be someone sitting in the car, in the front driver's seat. (Right-hand drive car).

In the first picture, which was taken front on, there appears to be a man with a frizzy afro style hair-do sitting in the driver's seat.

The next picture that was taken of the right-hand side, seems to show a younger, thinner man wearing a baseball cap.

I showed copies of the pictures to Kevin and his wife, who could both also see the man sitting in the car, and the property was blessed and given a cleansing ceremony the very next day.

Anyway, the auction proceeded and the vehicle was purchased by a Ford collector in Sydney.

It took two different interstate transporters to finally get the car loaded for its Interstate trip, as the car just would not budge when the time came. Eventually, the car was delivered to its new owner, but not until after two hours of trying to unload it off the truck.

It was not simply a case of locked on brakes or being stuck in gear, the car just refused to move and had to be winched off.

The new owner called me to say he was still very happy with the car and planned to set about restoring the rare vehicle.

About three days after hearing the car had been delivered in Sydney, I received a phone call from a private investigator. The investigator worked for an insurance company.

He advised me that only a couple of hours after being delivered, the car had totally disappeared from the buyer's driveway. Of course, we both believed the car must have just been stolen.

But the dilemma was that the car was almost impossible to move, had been parked and locked in a private driveway with two large metal gates securing the yard.

When the owner returned from just a quick trip up the road, he came back to find the gates still locked, but the car missing. The car was only insured for the amount of purchase, which was reasonably low and the owner would have to pay an excess to claim on the policy, meaning he would lose the big Interstate delivery charge and not recover all he paid to purchase it.

As a motor dealer, I am able to check the title and registration status of that vehicle.

It was never seen again.

This was not the only time someone was seen sitting in one of the cars I was asked to sell.

It was around 2014 I think and I was just locking up the house to get ready to go to bed.

I often bring our cat, Theo, in to sleep indoors at night and would often find him asleep lying on top of one of the cars in our driveway. We get a good view of the driveway from the large window in the kitchen.

This particular night I just looked out the kitchen window to see where "Theodore" was.

It was around 10:45 pm.

As I did, I could see what looked like someone sitting in the front seat of one of the cars straight in front of me.

It was like a black shadowy figure of a person sitting in this particular car, which had just been delivered that morning, for me to list for sale.

I must have stared at it for a good 10 seconds or more and there was no movement at all, so I just put it down to being the shape of the headrest and seat shoulders in the dark. I didn't go out to check, as I was only in underwear at the time, so I shrugged it off and went to bed.

The next morning, Marilou brought me in a cup of coffee and we chatted for a minute or two about our day ahead.

She then asked me: "Who was that sitting in the car last night?". I got goosebumps at hearing that, as I thought I had just been seeing something quite normal.

When I quizzed Marilou, she said she had got up around 11:30 pm to take a tablet, which she had forgotten to take.

She also looked out to see where Theo was and saw the dark figure, presumably of a man, sitting in the front passenger seat of the Car. She assumed I had someone come over to see the car in the dark, which believe it or not, is quite common in the used car game.

I bolted out of bed and got dressed, and then proceeded straight to the car outside.

And I was half expecting to see the Stereo missing or Car vandalised, but no, it was still locked and appeared untouched. Upon checking inside, everything was perfect.

I had to put it down to being the shape of the headrests and seat playing tricks on us.

But that night, I waited for it to get dark so I could check the inside silhouette of the car in the dark.

All I can say is, once dark, and without it being moved at all, the car looked nothing like it had the night before. There was nothing remotely looking like a figure sitting in the car. The headrests weren't even the same shape, not by a long shot.

For as many nights as that vehicle sat there, it never looked anything like it did on that first strange night.

Previous Page: The Ghost Car. When I took these pictures, there was no-one around and nobody was sitting in the Car. I can see a Man clearly sitting in the Driver's seat (RHD), and he appears to have Afro type Hair-do. He is transparent.

Above: Same Vehicle, taken just seconds later, there appears to be someone different sitting in the same position. This time wearing a T-Shirt with Vest and wearing a Cap.

CHAPTER 16

THE CEMETERY VISIT

As I mentioned earlier in the Chapter named "Danielle, My Daughter", Danni had been to a certain local cemetery in our area with her school friend Montana.

It was here that Danni had seen, what we believe, was the ghost of a lady who said "Hello" to Danielle, while her friend Montana saw nothing.

After hearing about this ghostly incident, I had been thinking about going there with Danni to see if we could get anything to happen again. It was a good 18 months later in 2018 that I happened to be passing the area with Danni as I was dropping her off at a friend's birthday party.

Later, after I had dropped her off, I was heading back home the same way and was just about to pass the road to the Cemetery, when I got the urge to take the turnoff and just go there, on my own. It was a perfectly bright sunny Saturday morning and I had nothing else planned.

I passed Montana's place and turned the corner

around into the Cemetery.

There was a great feeling of peace as I pulled up outside, parked the car and then very casually approached the graves on foot.

It wasn't all that often I went to Cemeteries really, maybe every couple of years or so, but this time I just wanted to try something I had heard about before.

Someone had told me that if you ask those spirits present to "Show you something", you would often get an immediate response. So quickly, it is almost as if they could pre-empt your question or request. I knew I had to give this a try.

I thought I would just stroll slowly and quietly past each grave, stopping momentarily at each one to say their names, one after the other, in my mind.

I did this for quite a few minutes, while observing and listening for any signs of a presence. I had never quite done this before, not paying as much attention as on this outing, and thought I would just observe.

When I got down to the last row of graves, I only had about another 20 or so to go before reaching the end of that section. I then stopped in front of the third or fourth grave in that bottom row and then said very gently, with a weak voice: "Show Me Something".

Almost immediately, and I mean within three seconds, 2 beautiful Butterflies came up from behind the headstone of the grave immediately to my right.

They quickly appeared in front of me and buzzed around my head several times, before eventually flying off together to my left. They were out of sight in just a matter of ten seconds or so.

I was pleased to get such an immediate result, and it was quite amazing to see, but I wanted to experience more as proof to myself. So I said "Thank You" to acknowledge that I had received this confirmation and walked along passed another few graves.

When I was about 8 graves along the final row, I again asked: "What else can you show me? Once again, and I mean right on cue, an even more beautiful blue-winged butterfly came up from behind the headstone, which was again located immediately to my right.

This time the butterfly landed on the flowers on the grave right in front of me and it just sat there, for it seemed, as long as I wanted to look at it.

I have spent almost 50 years living in Australia, with 38 years living in Queensland. I have never seen such beautiful butterflies as the ones I saw that day. Even living in the immediate area for 26 years, I have not seen the likes of those butterflies ever before.

But this was not quite the end, for the finale was yet to come.

Once again I said: "Thank You, Thank You for

showing me".

Before moving on from that spot and with the butterfly still content to just sit there on the wilting flowers, with an occasional open and closing of its wings, I decided to have a good look around for any other butterflies that might be hanging around.

Despite having a good look all around me, there wasn't another butterfly to be seen anywhere.

Being thankful for the pleasant experience I had received so far, I thought I would try my luck with a third and final request.

As I walked down to the last two or three graves in that back row, I stood there and asked: "Can you show me anything else?".

All of a sudden, as if I had commanded it, a very strong gust of wind appeared and blew straight through the grass and trees located just 20 or 30 feet behind the graves.

The grass was bending over almost flat and the trees bent heavily with leaves and branches snapping off. It came and was gone in less than about ten seconds.

There were no gusts of wind before or after that happened, just a lovely still and sunny day. The power that was shown in that display was awe-inspiring.

I had the feeling that I was not dealing with just the one spirit, but a collective force that was watching me and had possibly even been waiting for me.

I now increased my speed of walking and made my way out of there at a much faster pace than I had entered.

CHAPTER 17
THE DAGUERREOTYPE PICTURE

I guess that I first developed a love of Antiques, and even better, Antiquities when I was only quite a young boy.

I remember when Mum would take me to an old market in Ross-on-Wye, in Herefordshire, England back in 1977 when I was about nine years old. The Market has been there since medieval times.

There were plastic ice cream containers full of old coins for sale, some even from Ancient Roman times and I would spend ages going through them all to find something rare or valuable.

I was fascinated by the boxes of old post cards and the stamp collections on display, alongside the antique photographs and books. The history I saw there for the first time was wonderful and I couldn't get enough of it.

Later on in life, I also became a secondhand dealer at the markets and art galleries, selling all sorts of goods which eventually I transitioned into the antique's trade. I have done so on and off for over 25 years now, while at one stage it was my main source of business for almost 10 years. It wasn't so much the antique furniture that took my fancy, but ceramics, art, bric-a-brac and collectables.

Having always had an interest in photography, I also loved looking at old photos from bygone eras.

The one thing that always fascinated me the most though, was Daguerreotype Pictures.

If you are not familiar with Daguerreotype's, they are the first real photographs as such, using a photo developing procedure and technique invented by Frenchman Louis Daguerre in the late 1830's.

By the 1840's, popularity spread and people could now have an affordable picture taken of themselves and thousands of photographic studios would eventually be set up around the world. Before this time, people would have to commission a painting to be done of them, which was often expensive, took a great deal of time and the results could vary greatly.

What I find most fascinating about the Daguerreotype process, is the fact that the sitter would actually pose in front of a wooden box camera that held a highly polished silver mirror inside and the person's image would be developed on to the mirror plate. Imagine looking into a mirror and having your reflection frozen for eternity or at least for the very long life of the picture. That is what you are looking at when you see a Daguerreotype picture, the person's actual reflection frozen in the mirror.

This is quite amazing, yet creepy as most of these pictures are now 170 years old or so, at time of writing and their image can still be seen crisply and with a lot of clarity that is often lacking from later printed photographs, which are just a printed facsimile of the original picture taken.

So the Daguerreotype is a very personal item because the plate which has been developed and framed was actually in the Camera, just a few feet away usually and right in front of the sitter at the time the picture was taken. The finished picture was also placed in a folding case and gilt frame that was often chosen by the person or their family. Most contain a beautiful velvet or silk lining and were often handled by the person in the picture. Some may contain a lock of hair too. Also many Daguerreotype's consist of pictures of the Dead. These are known as Memento Mori.

To be able to touch, smell and examine the portrait up close after all these years is quite an amazing experience. Yes, even smell them, because they can give off a fragrant smell that is the essence of time itself.

I have owned quite a few examples over the years and I have always delighted in seeing them.

The unfortunate thing about being a dealer in antiques, classic cars, collectables and so on, is that we often have to part with a lot of our favourite items just to keep going in our business.

It was only in 2018 that I saw a nice little "Dag" for sale on eBay and it was going ever so cheap, so I bought the item.

It is a picture of a young boy about six to eight years old dressed in a Count of Monte Cristo cape and outfit. It has a "CMC" monogram embroidered on the cuffs of the boy's costume as well.

It took my eye because it was in a rare George Washington case and the subject matter was interesting. When I received it in the mail from the USA, I removed the framed glass plate from the case to inspect it and saw someone had inscribed the date 1860 inside.

It must have sat neatly wrapped up in my sock drawer for about three months until I started thinking about it again constantly. I would take it out and look at it every couple of weeks or so and then put it back in the drawer.

One day I was at home on my own and was doing a bit of tidying up and putting some clothes away when I came across the picture once more. I took it out of the cloth it was wrapped in and just sat on the bed looking at it. At that point, I felt like I needed to rest and I laid down on the bed grasping the picture in my left hand.

I remember saying to myself mentally that I would love to be taken back to the day in 1860 when that picture was taken to just see what it was like. I also thought to myself that I would definitely go if I had the chance. Not long after, maybe a couple of minutes at most, I drifted off into this very realistic dream-like state, while semi-awake, that had me feeling very much like I had been transported back to that very time.

Suddenly I found myself standing by a wooden building. It had not long been built, as the timber was still wet and green and I could also smell the freshly sawn timber. I could see an old-style black hurricane lamp hanging off the wooden beam above me. There was an unsealed yellow coloured gravel road right in front of me with wheel grooves and potholes in it. The air was fragrant with flowers and the foliage from a nearby pine forest.

I could also smell smoke, tar, horse manure and something like creosote for preserving timber. There was a low roaring sound that can only be described as the sound of the Earth turning. As I thought to myself that I should walk down the street a bit, I could feel myself float forward, while hovering maybe six inches above the ground. At this stage, I was thinking it was time for me to snap out of it, but I so much wanted to see more.

As I projected forwards a few feet, I could see that the wooden structure I had been standing near was a very basic railway station building. The building itself and the gravel road were quite new. As I looked up the street, I could see three colonial-style wooden houses to the left, all painted white and on the right side of the road were a couple of plain wooden buildings that looked like stables or workshops.

The most obvious thing to me was just how quiet it was, although I could hear what sounded like a blacksmith banging a hammer in one of the wooden buildings to my right. I decided to move a bit further up the street and at will seemed to float past the first house on my left and turned to face the second house. It had a very low, matt white picket fence and a flower garden that was heavily overgrown with long grasses and weeds. I passed through the little front gate that was already open and hanging off its hinges and approached what was like a flywire door. As I entered the house by floating through the wire door and then the main door that was wide open, I was seen by a wire-haired mongrel dog that noticed me, but slightly cowered and took a step back before giving a little growl as it stared at me. It was white with tan patches and of medium size. I could smell smoke and see sooty walls in the entrance of the house and saw well-used candles on enamelled metal holders nailed to the wall.

At this stage I thought to myself that the detail in this dream was all too real and that I had better end it now. I really felt as if I was haunting someone else's house, in the past.

Nothing happened at first, I just felt myself hovering off the floor, feeling about six and a half feet tall off the ground, which is six inches taller than my actual height. I had the strange feeling that time was passing in slow motion and that I may even get stuck there.

Now thinking about coming out of it again, I said in my mind that I wanted to go back.

With that, I found myself back near the railway station office once more for a few seconds and then finally came out of my dream-like state. What seemed like only three minutes at my destination, I found I was out to it for 40 minutes at this end.

We have all had dreams many times. Usually, they are somewhat hazy and forgettable at best, but this one that I asked for was so realistic and totally memorable down to the last detail. I can remember it in far more detail than my last overseas holiday.

I do not believe I was asleep at any stage of this adventure but in a sort of semi-conscious state.

Just like at the Cemetery, I simply asked in my mind to be shown something and I was shown it.

I still can't really explain what happened that day.

The actual 1860 Daguerreotype of a young boy that took me on a very vivid and real Astral Travel, which I believe showed me the day and place that the picture was taken, just as I had asked to be shown.

CHAPTER 18
CONCLUSION

W hen I set out to write this book, which is the first book I have written and published, my intention was simply to tell of the amazing and uncanny occurrences that were experienced by me and those around me.

Nothing has changed. This book was never intended to change anyone's views on the subject, interfere with a person's religious beliefs or to push my own beliefs onto anyone else.

It was just that having been witness to so many instances of the paranormal, that I feel it is one's duty to reveal, explain and discuss the subject.

For what has happened to me and my family is too amazing to just keep quiet about.

And I say this knowing that many readers will no doubt have their own spooky stories to tell on the subject.

For as many people as I have told about even just one occurrence, they often come back to me with a similar, if not more amazing experience they had themselves.

In this day of information and technology, there can

hardly be a more worthy subject to investigate than Life After Death. I mean, almost none of us hope that when we die, that is it, that we are dead forever. And although this life can seem long and tiring, very stressful and with much sadness and pain, it may not be until we actually die, that we really start to live.

Along the way though, I have picked up some of my own beliefs and also made observations that kind of give us some sort of understanding of what is possibly going on.

I would like to share this information with you now, but of course, it is up to you to form your own judgements and opinions and I will fully respect that.

1. I believe that we all have a soul, and that our soul survives death.

2. It is a separate part from our physical body, resides in the body during our physical lifetime and it continues as normal after the death of our mortal body. The soul is us, and it is our true being, our character and connection to the creator. We were born with this soul, were with it before we were born and will have it after death. It resides in the physical body somewhere between the solar plexus and head region.

3. The soul enters the body immediately before the mother starts to feel her baby kick for the first time. It is the gravity, heat, heavy weight, wetness,

the feeling of suffocation and restriction that causes the soul to react somewhat violently when it enters the mother's body for the first time. Before that, it was free to float about quite effortlessly.

4. Before our soul arrived at the physical body and entered our mother's body to occupy a living foetus, for all intents and purposes, we were already dead. We were existing only as a soul in spirit form, just like we think of those who have passed over, so really we have already been dead before we were born, and it was nothing to be afraid of. We have been there before and it was our home. It's where we came from.

5. The reason we are here, or the meaning of life if you wish, is to experience life in a physical body. Before we were born, we were devoid of almost all the earthbound experiences that one can experience with a physical body. For example: Being able to breathe the air, taste the fruits of this world, to smell the flowers, feel the touch of another being, feel the Earth under your feet, experience the physical feelings of love and pain, joy and sadness, make physical bodies for other souls to inhabit and just simply to experience life on Earth in a physical body.

6. The ones most likely to be able to communicate with those on the other side are children, the sick and those who have attuned themselves to the idea

that communication with spirits is possible. Children because they have recently come from the other side, they were there most recently out of all of us. As kids often have not yet been told such things are wrong or impossible, they are a lot more open to receiving visits and messages. Those who are sick and dying can have one foot in the grave, so to speak and may start to see those on the other side. It is not unusual for them to be visited by passed loved ones, hear beautiful music from the other side and even be given times and dates of when they may cross over. And like children, those of any age who are open to the idea of being able to receive communication or confirmation from the other side can and usually will start to have experiences. You just have to be open to the idea and be observant.

7. My experience seems to be that you will receive a visit either when you least expect it or soon after the time when a person has passed. Most of my experiences came completely out of the blue or within a short period of time of a loved one crossing over. It will usually take you quite by surprise and you may not even notice the relevance of it until later.

8. There seems to be some sort of laws in place that spirits must abide by. One seems to be that they must try to keep out of sight of the living. I often catch something out of the corner of my eye that

disappears as soon as I turn. Often, they will not make contact with you unless you make contact or invite them first. Spirits seem to also come back for special occasions, especially birthdays and anniversaries. In our house, we always light a couple of candles in the evening to remember birthdays of those who have passed and can sometimes feel their presence. Wedding anniversaries and remembering a person on the anniversary of their death or funeral can also seem to bring about a visit from that person.

9. Spirits can gain strength and make themselves aware to you by using electricity or appliances. It seems that when leaving a TV, PC or Radio on with just static playing, you may get a voice come through from the other side, by using the static as a carrier. As proof of origin, they will often call your name. As mentioned before, this happened to me with a clock radio that was just off station. It also appears that spirits can cause lights to flicker, batteries to drain, bulbs to pop and areas to turn cold. My brother Rod once had a touch lamp that would answer questions by flickering once or twice with each question.

10. Travelling the world seems to be no problem for those on the other side, as they are not bound by the same earthly confines that we suffer, such as distance, gravity, time or money. I believe they can travel from England to Australia, for example, or anywhere else in just the blink of an eye, or

more likely- just by thinking about it. When I had a visit from Mum in Australia one afternoon, she was also seen standing by my sister's bed in the morning in England, which was less than about an hour apart.

11. I believe all people and especially animals have psychic ability. Many people have just forgotten how or have chosen not to use it. But it can be activated again at any age and developed. There are fake psychics out there, who will do almost anything to make money or make a name for themselves, and there are many with real gifts who charge nothing at all. I am not against a person who is genuine charging for their services, people need to live. It's no different to visiting the hairdresser really, they provide a service and if it helps you- how much is that worth? It can take a lot to sort the wheat from the chaff, but those with genuine abilities will often stand out as the real deal. The two psychic's that really stood out to me as being totally real were Marce and another lady called Maureen. Neither ever charged anybody a cent. But here is something you may not have thought of. I have met a few psychic's who worked professionally as grief or youth councillors. They use their abilities and intuition to help people, without ever telling anyone what they were doing, that made them so good at their job.

12. It doesn't seem to matter whether a person is buried in the ground, buried at sea or cremated. It also seems to make little difference in how the person died. Regardless of how a person died, or the type of funeral, that's if they had a funeral at all, they all seem to be able to come back equally. One of my Grandfathers was lost at sea, my other Grandfather was Cremated. Both appeared and were standing beside Mum's bed before she passed. Peter was buried, Mum was cremated. Both came back multiple times and with great strength. I do however feel that those who had a horrific death may remember their passing, but rest assured there is absolutely no pain now. Also, a person is returned to perfect form and health on the other side, so there is no blindness or deafness, no missing limbs or scars or burns. Just a memory of the experience.

13. I am often asked if I believe that these occurrences could be caused by demons who are trying to fool us. There is always that possibility, but I don't quite believe it. I would expect that if a demon or bad spirit was trying to fool you, and yes there are bad spirits out there, then the intention for that trickery would be to confuse or deceive people or get them to turn their backs on religion. But having these experiences tends to drive people towards a belief in God or a Creator and many turn to religion or become more spiritual as a result. So

the intended purpose of confusing people doesn't work, as many atheists who experience a supernatural encounter start to reconsider their belief in there being nothing at all. You can be fooled by playful spirits, who were once just people who lived like us, but when your loved one shows up, you will know when it is them.

14. Not only Humans have Souls, but all living creatures. Especially Cats and Dogs, who are on a similar plain to us and are often waiting for us on the other side or come back and make their presence known to us after they have died. You can expect to feel the weight of your deceased pet jump up on the bed or sofa, or feel something sit on your lap, see footprints on the floor or on furniture, or as happened to us, hear Meow's coming from the wall. When a friend of mine called Archie died and was brought back to life after being dead for eight and a half minutes, he said his pet Dogs he had as a child in Scotland were there waiting for him, as well as other family members who had passed. Archie was so adamant about his near death experience, that he spent the rest of his life telling everyone he met about it. When he eventually died the second time, he had left specific instructions that he not be revived again. He so wanted to go back.

15. On the subject of Near Death Experiences, or NDE's as they are called, I have met several

people who have explained to me what they saw after they died. The stories are all similar and share a common theme of seeing their life flash before them, seeing and going towards the light and being met by deceased loved ones or even God. Some scientists will say this is just the body shutting down and giving you a review of your life, to sort of calm you down and prepare you for death. I could sort of agree with that I guess, but it doesn't explain why some people come back from the dead with supernatural powers or knowledge of future events or even a complete change in personality. I met a man called Archie on Russell Island about 2005 or 2006. At the time when he died in an accident, he was the person who spent the longest time dead, to be revived in Australia. He claimed to have spent about an hour on the other side, although he was only gone for eight and a half minutes and saw a beautiful golden city on the other side of beautiful fields of wheat. As I said before, he was met by his deceased family members from Scotland and even his childhood dogs. But Archie returned a different man. He became a high level football player for a major team, became a great guitarist who travelled overseas with a famous band, raised over a million dollars for a charity in the 1980's by running over 3000 kms and much more. He achieved all of this in later life, after he had died and come back. His deceased Family relatives at first greeted him as if he was there to stay, but eventually were advised they had to send him back.

16. If the brain was just showing him a life review when he died, it must have been some very impressive movie indeed.

17. I don't think it is safe to use such things as Ouija Boards, Spirit Boards, Seances and the like. They can get you great results but can be dangerous. They need to be opened and closed properly and there is no certainty that something won't attach to you or your home. I don't really dabble in such things myself, and as you know, I have still achieved some amazing results without even trying. It is possible that things such as EMF readers or Spirit Voice Boxes etc. may be ok as tools, but one still needs to be very careful. I think genuine friendly spirits of family and friends will make themselves known to you without any sort of apparatus.

18. We need to be aware of the little signs to watch out for, that are sent to us when loved ones try to make contact. I myself have experienced finding random small coins left around the place, seen butterflies appear from nowhere, have friendly moths sit on the wall for a long period of time or buzz around me, have random birds come down to me and hang around, hear that special song on the

radio at the right time and find other small trinkets or signs about the place. This may not make any sense to some people, but as you start to hone your sensory skills, you will start to spot little indicators appearing. When Marilou's good friend died unexpectedly, Marilou had this beautiful Moth that looked like a big bumblebee keep following her around the hotel rooms that she was working in. It looked like a cross between a butterfly and a wasp. It would sit on the walls right near her and follow her around the building. It was quite big and coloured bright yellow and black. At that same time, she had just heard on Facebook that her good friend had died in the Philippines. She always wore black with yellow stripes and dressed like a bee. My Mum always liked the hymn "Ave Maria". Right at the time of her passing, the radio station I was listening to played a very haunting version of Ave Maria. Afterwards, the DJ said he doesn't usually play stuff like that but hoped that someone out there enjoyed it. It is hard to explain some of the possible scenarios, but keep an eye or ear out for strange coincidences.

19. Buildings, places, cars and even some objects can be haunted. If they were loved or hated by those who occupied or owned them first, they may contain residual energy or still be frequented or possessed by those who have an attachment. So there really are haunted houses, battlefields,

hospitals, asylums, jewellery and cars etc. I have previously mentioned the ghost car we had picked up. When I moved my Dad into a retirement Village last year, a friendly young aged care worker was there to meet and greet us. Without me even saying a word on this subject, she informed me that almost all of the rooms were haunted as they had many previous occupants pass away in them. She told me she herself had seen ghosts walking the corridors and many seemed to be unaware they were dead. She even recognised one man who had recently passed. I was quite shocked at her frank admission, but I knew she was right. I still feel it too when I visit my Dad.

20. When you hear little kids talking to someone who isn't there or your dog or cat seems to be seeing, hearing or staring at something you cannot see, you are probably having a visit. For the most part, this is not something to fear unless your child cries or the dog barks or growls or the cat hisses. It may, however, be a good opportunity to ask questions of the child or be observant for things like doors opening or closing on their own, or pictures moving on the wall. If you have a camera handy, try to take pictures or video of the general area and ask for confirmation of someone being there. You may get orbs to appear in the pictures or video or even hear a knock on the wall. Always acknowledge and thank them afterwards. Don't be afraid, they are

still going to visit you whether you are aware of it or not.

21. Between the hours of Midnight to around 4am, there can be an increase in other worldly phenomena. This is because the veil that separates this world and the next is at its thinnest around that time and the world around you is darker and quiet, making it easier to notice sounds, lights, footsteps, knocks etc. You can expect to have more occurrences take place during these times than at other times, however, things can happen at anytime, it's just more prolific during those hours.

22. Try to trust your gut feelings and instincts about things. We were born with a conscience and many senses. Your conscience is there to keep you from doing wrong to others, to protect your soul, and your senses and instincts are there to protect you from harm. Women are a lot more in tune to this than men usually. We have all heard of Women's Intuition. But I often get an inkling about something, like: "don't go in there", "that doesn't feel right", "look under here", "move out of the way", "something's about to happen", "I don't like the sound of that", "I don't trust that person", "I don't feel I should go". These warnings can often be inspired by passed loved ones who are guiding us. They can be premonitions of future events, so stay in tune and be aware. Learn to trust your intuition.

CLOSING WORDS

I hope this book has been of some interest to you all and I feel really honoured you took the time to read some of my uncanny ghostly stories.

The contents of this book are totally True, happened to me and my family and I have described them to the best of my knowledge and abilities.

This book has attracted a lot of interest in pre-sale and I have already received enquiries as to whether there will be another follow-up book.

I would consider releasing another book on this subject if I can gather more True Accounts, but this time from the public at large.

This new book will probably be called:

"More Evidence for Life After Death".

If you wish to share your True Stories with me for consideration of having them published in my next book, I would be very pleased to hear from you.

You can message me at: evidencebook@dodo.com.au

Love and Peace,
Darren Perks
January, 2020

UPDATE 2021

W ell it's been an interesting last 12 Months to say the least. With Covid affecting the entire Planet and Lockdown after Lockdown, I guess we are lucky to have survived so far. But most of us are still here and must go on celebrating life itself.

There have been a few updates since writing this book 13 Months ago. (While on the cusp of going into the first Lockdown). My Brother in Law, Maurice (Mauri), who is Jen's Partner passed away from cancer in the second half of 2020. It was a long time coming and we were expecting it, but it was still very sad and has been hard on Jen.

Also, last year, after over 13 Years of waiting, the Family finally got together to scatter both Mum's and Vanda's Ashes together in the Bay, near Brisbane. It was both a sombre, yet also somewhat heartwarming affair and it is quite surreal to see the remains of both your Mother and Sister being poured out into the Water.

Mum was a Water Sign, Pisces, so she would have loved that. I kept Mum's Ashes at Home for 13 Years and didn't know what to do with them. I mean, they weren't mine to just scatter as I wished, as there are many other Family Members wishes to consider. But when Vanda passed away and Her ashes were to be scattered where her Son Aidan had his ashes scattered, it seemed sensible to free Mum's ashes at the same time.

Since that time, there has been a lot less spiritual activity in our home and it feels so much more at ease. I guess Mum really needed to be finally laid to rest in peace.

I hope you enjoy the Pictures I have now added to the Book. It does make things a little bit easier to visualise when you can see images of what I have been talking about.

And a big Thank You to those who have messaged Me about their encounters. I have really enjoyed hearing them. One was about a nine year old Girl in England who saw a Medieval Ghost dressed in old chain male and metal helmet, whilst touring an old Castle.

I would still love to hear more of Your stories.

Kindest Regards,

Darren Perks.

Printed in Great Britain
by Amazon